The Spiritual Runes

A Guide to the Ancestral Wisdom

First published by O Books, 2009
O Books is an imprint of John Hunt Publishing Ltd., The Bothy, Deershot Lodge, Park Lane, Ropley,
Hants, SO24 0BE, UK
office1@o-books.net
www.o-books.net

Distribution in:

UK and Europe
Orca Book Services
orders@orcabookservices.co.uk
Tel: 01202 665432 Fax: 01202 666219
Int. code (44)

USA and Canada
NBN
custserv@nbnbooks.com
Tel: 1 800 462 6420 Fax: 1 800 338 4550

Australia and New Zealand
Brumby Books
sales@brumbybooks.com.au
Tel: 61 3 9761 5535 Fax: 61 3 9761 7095

Far East (offices in Singapore, Thailand,
Hong Kong, Taiwan)
Pansing Distribution Pte Ltd
kemal@pansing.com
Tel: 65 6319 9939 Fax: 65 6462 5761

South Africa
Alternative Books
altbook@peterhyde.co.za
Tel: 021 555 4027 Fax: 021 447 1430

Text copyright Harmonia Saille 2008

Design: Stuart Davies

ISBN: 978 1 84694 201 3

A CIP catalogue record for this book is available
from the British Library.

Printed by Digital Book Print

O Books operates a distinctive and ethical publishing philosophy in
all areas of its business, from its global network of authors to
production and worldwide distribution.
This book is produced on FSC certified stock, within ISO14001
standards. The printer plants sufficient trees each year through
the Woodland Trust to absorb the level of emitted carbon in
its production.

The Spiritual Runes

A Guide to the Ancestral Wisdom

Harmonia Saille

BOOKS

Winchester, UK
Washington, USA

CONTENTS

To Mum
Lilian Margaret Hughes
28 February 1929 – 14 February 2005
Forever our Valentine

Acknowledgments

I would like to start by thanking my lovely husband Rick for all his help, unfailing faith and never-ending support. My children, Glenn, Owen, Rosemarie, James and Mikey, and stepchildren, Sarina, Rick Merlin, Tanya, and Joëlle also deserve thanks for their comments and believing in me (and who will surely complain if I don't mention them all by name). My heartfelt thanks go to my lovely stepfather Gareth Hughes (Gaz), my brothers and sisters, especially Diane Marelli who kindly bullied me, and Frances Edge whose humor kept me going. Special thanks go to my dear friend the late Dr Edmund Cusick, for our many discussions on the runes, and also to Jenny Newman and friends at Liverpool John Moores University School of Writing and School of English, for their teaching and faith, and for giving me that extra courage and confidence. More special thanks go to author Cassandra Eason who with her wonderful books started me off on my magical quest. Thank you to Hermijn Smit who suggested I teach the runes and to Debby Potters-Bolung for starting me off with my workshops, and to all the students who attended for their general input. My first students deserve special mentions, Samantha van den Heiligenberg, Louise Looy, Maaike Steenstra, Kim Tolboom, Debby, and Maria Zingoni for their bind rune suggestions, along with Annemarie Rozema, Nancy Gerritzen, and Jolanda Klaver-Olsman, for all their helpful comments, and not to forget Ellen Knoops and Samanthi for their help too. And special mentions go to Krystina, Kaddy, and all my other wonderful friends in the UK and The Netherlands who supported me. Last but not least, my grateful thanks to my oldest and dearest friend, psychic Beryl Weston who predicted the book and for her lasting faith and encouragement.

Introduction

When I embarked on my study of the runes and runelore I found it to be a much more complex business than I expected. I soon realized that unraveling the threads of knowledge required for communication with the runes in a committed way, would take intensive study. And even after that lengthy study and research, I came to see that there would always be something new to discover about them. What really struck me was the connection I came to have with them, like that of a trusted friend. My rune stones, which I diligently collected from a riverbank and inscribed, blessed, and empowered with the potent silver light of the full moon, became part of my life. A bond of trust formed between us and though on occasions I did not like what they were telling me, I appreciated the wisdom of them.

Over time, the symbols came to mean more to me than just signs that anyone can read the meanings of in books. They became a secret language, each symbol telling me over and beyond anything I could ever read about. I had made a connection with them on a spiritual level.

To help you gain an overall insight into how the runes work, I have written an introductory course. In doing so, I arranged the course of study in what I decided was a coherent manner in order to unravel those threads of knowledge somewhat, and provide the basic knowledge required to becoming a runecaster. For after that, only regular use and experience will further your acquaintance with them and lead you forward to becoming a "runemaster". Moreover, and perhaps significantly, I hope to lead you, the seeker of wisdom, in gaining that all-important spiritual connection with the runes, and guide you on your way to recognizing your own subliminal inner being, just as ultimately, the runes will guide you on a journey of self-discovery.

How the Course Works

First we will acquaint ourselves with the runes. For once we know how they came to be, their history and traditions, we can start to form a bond with them just as we do when we become familiar with that trusted friend.

Over time, the runes underwent several transformations to fit in with the people of particular periods in history, their beliefs and religions, and hence there are now several traditions. The tradition I talk about in this book is what is known as The Elder Futhark, and is the oldest known rune tradition.

If we look at the study of runes as a tree in which it branches off into three main boughs, each an "aett" of eight runes, then to get to them we need to climb the tree. To do this in a practical way we have to travel slowly from the roots up the trunk until we reach the boughs. The roots are the many threads of knowledge connecting ourselves with the runes, and the trunk is the bridge linking the two. For in the boughs are the runes themselves, and to be able to understand and connect with them, it is necessary to learn the basic history, mythology, philosophy, psychology, and meanings of them. Then there is the practical side too in their making, casting, and magical use. There are eight Chapters in this book as the number eight has magical significance, for instance each aett has eight runes.

I know that many people embarking on the study of the runes, will in their eagerness and enthusiasm miss almost all the roots out, and having quickly learnt the meanings rush straight to the top of the tree. You will have heard of the saying "out on a limb". Well, this metaphor is appropriate here. If you rush to the top of the tree without much thought of what you are doing, then you might find yourself out on a limb where you are exposed to difficulties. You will soon encounter something you do not understand. You will possibly be asked questions you cannot answer and you will have to climb down again to find the answers. And if you do not listen to your intuition and go even further along the limb, you risk the bough breaking and will lose interest altogether. It really is better to learn everything we can in order to cross the trunk-bridge confidently knowing that we are familiar with our runes. This will take time, and by putting in the extra effort, you will be sure to reap the rewards.

I would propose then beginning at the roots of the tree, and I recommend additional study over and above the information I provide.

It is always wise to buy more than one book when studying a complex subject such as the runes. But surely, you may ask, one book is much the same as another. Well, you can buy a simple book on rune meanings along with a rune set. I would avoid these or at least buy some books to go with it that cover everything relating to the runes, not just their meanings. There are some books criticized as being inaccurate, but they remain extremely popular because people find something to relate to in their contents. And then there are some books which are perhaps too academic for some seekers, who would rather begin in a more basic way. Therefore, I have taken a middle road in writing this book.

Whichever way you wish to tackle it, books on the runes are subjective and depend on the approach of the author. We all became skilled in different ways and so have our own slant on how the runes should be studied. Consequently, guidebooks are often about personal journeys of discovery that worked well and which the author wants to share with others, and that is what I am doing in writing this book.

Many of you will already have a set of runes, perhaps bought, or have been given as a present, or have already made a set. If you wish to continue using this set then you will find ways of making them more personal in Chapter 6. You will also require a set of runes for the visualization exercises in Chapters 3 and 4. You can leave these exercises until you have acquired a set. Otherwise if you already have a set, but perhaps have decided to make your own in addition at some point, then these can be used in the meantime.

Throughout this book when I use the terms "runecaster" and "runemaster", I refer to both the female and male.

Chapter 1

The Runes and Their History

What Are the Runes?

When I am asked to do a reading for someone, one thing they often ask is "What are the runes?" and often they add, "Are they like the tarot?" so I give them a brief explanation of the runes, to enable them to understand a little better how their reading works. I also explain how I will cast them and what their own role will be. Always for a reading, I set the scene and mood. A calm, relaxed, and most of all, peaceful atmosphere, is essential for a good connection. Outdoors is ideal.

One day I went into a bookshop and saw that there were people giving tarot readings with many other people milling about, some shopping and some hanging around curious to see what was happening. For me personally, this would not be a satisfactory way to read the runes. The tarot is an excellent form of divination and one that I regularly use, but I believe the runes have to be treated in a different way simply because they are different. Some runecasters do like to treat the two forms of divination the same, using them at a table. There are others who compare the runes directly with the tarot, matching each rune with a particular card and sometimes tending to give them the same meanings and emphasis. If this works personally for them then there is no reason to suppose it invalid. As time goes by, everything evolves or changes to fit the times. But I believe each form of divination benefits from having its own processes and rituals, and so I choose to treat the runes and tarot as differently as I would a crystal ball or the *I Ching*, and prefer not to make comparisons.

The runes are an ancient alphabet which was used not only for communicating information in the way of writing short messages, but also for divination and magic. They were used chiefly in Britain, Scandinavia, Iceland, the Northern Netherlands, and North-west Germany. Yet, this is no ordinary script, for the runes not only have an ancient history behind them, but a wealth of mythology, and were originally the gift of Odin.

The word "rune" comes from the Old Germanic word *runa*, meaning secret or mystery. It is thought that the angular points in the runes symbols were designed to be used for carving, for instance into wood or stone. This simple method made it available to all who knew the rune symbols, for these materials were easily obtainable. In modern times, these natural materials are also easily obtainable and we can carve the runes for ourselves, just as in times past, and without cost.

In addition to its letter use in writing, each rune sign has an accompanying name and a symbolic meaning. The rune symbols have a connection with that meaning, but exactly what is not known, although there has been some conjecture. For instance, *Algiz* means the elk or elk sedge. It most likely represents the antlers of the elk or perhaps the sharp, spiky leaves of the elk sedge grass, but as it is a protection rune we could put our own emphasis on it. I call it the "guardian angel" rune. The fact that the letters were also given names indicates that they were used for magical purposes, perhaps even before their use as an alphabet.

In the past runemasters were held in high esteem. The runic symbols were transcribed onto rocks and other items. As well as used for writing, runes were etched onto the materials that were available at those times, probably wood or bone, for use as divinatory tools, magic and healing. Sadly, as runes used for divination were etched onto perishable materials, there are no examples left. Most rune inscriptions found have been carved on stone.

In modern times, the runes are carved, etched, or painted onto wood, stone, bone, pottery, or other natural materials (such as crystal). Homemade runes are generally made from wood or stone. They are used both as divinatory tools and as magical talismans. Sometimes the runes are used for writing spells or coded messages. As talismans, more than one rune, generally two or three, are put together and made into what is called a "bind rune". The runes chosen are ones that complement each other. As with all magic, components should not conflict, but blend and balance.

Perhaps you first heard of the runes from reading the books of J.R.R. Tolkien. He used a variant of the Anglo-Saxon runes for the dust jacket of *The Hobbit* and for the writing on *Thror's map*, after seeing them on a Viking longboat found in the River Thames. He then went on to invent his own rune languages for *The Lord of the Rings*. This has encouraged the growing popularity of the runes for divination and magic.

I have included below an archeologically and historical based record of the runes, as well as the mythology of the runes, as both are vital to our understanding.

Rune History Main Points

Rune script appears to have been in existence for around two thousand years, probably longer, perhaps from 200 bce. Rune script was used well into the Middle Ages on weapons, tools, jewelry, coins, stones, and even coffins and headstones.

It is speculated that the runic alphabet originated from the Etruscan alphabet in central Italy and was spread by merchants traveling through central Europe and as far as the Baltic Sea.

The historical sources, from which most of the information about the runes comes, are mythological and heroic "lays" most commonly the Eddas, the rune poems, archaeological finds (in the form of carvings on artifacts and stones), and early writers such as the Roman historian, Tacitus. Tacitus recorded an account of what is thought to be rune casting in the first century CE. In relation to divination and lot casting by the priest of the community, or father of the family, Tacitus wrote that a branch from a fruit-bearing tree is cut into small slices and marked with divinatory signs and scattered onto a white cloth. After evoking the gods, and with eyes lifted skywards, the caster picks up three pieces of wood and interprets them one at a time according to the symbols written upon them. You can learn more about a "Tacitus" style casting in Chapter 7.

The Principal Rune Rows

There are several different rune rows which came into being over the centuries, with many variations in number, spelling, and some differences in the way the symbols are drawn.

The Elder Futhark

The Elder Futhark, often called the Common Germanic Futhark, has 24 runes, and all other rune rows developed from this one.

The Elder Futhark is the oldest rune row and is thought to have come into use in about 100 CE. It is this Futhark that we will be discussing throughout this book.

The name "Futhark" is taken from the initial six runes of the first aett (set of eight runes) *Fehu* (F), *Uruz* (U), *Thurisaz* (Th), *Ansuz* (A), *Raidho* (R), and *Kenaz* (K).

There are three sets of eight runes in the Elder Futhark, collectively known as "aettir". They are named after three gods: the first aett is named for Frey (though some writers attribute it to the goddess Freyja, and some to both), the second is the god Hagal (though what is known about him is generally surmised), and the third is the god Tyr. Developments in language caused The Elder Futhark to be replaced by the Younger Futhark in about 800 CE.

The Anglo-Saxon/Anglo-Frisian Runes

The Anglo-Saxon /Anglo-Frisian rune set (a Northumbrian set originated from these too) has 28 runes although some variants have more. Around the late fifth or early sixth century, the runic alphabet in Friesland, in the northern Netherlands, developed further to accommodate new sounds. This was owing to radical changes in the language, and as a result of this, four new letters were added. It was this rune row that was taken to Britain by Saxon invaders. There it developed further and the various rune rows that evolved from this increased to as many as 33 runes.

The Anglo-Frisian or Anglo-Saxon runes became a "Futhorc" reflecting the changes in sounds. It was most likely in the ninth century that the Northumbrian runes, derived from the Anglo-Saxon runes, increased to 33 runes.

The Younger Futhark

The Viking or Scandinavian rune script known as the Younger Futhark has only 16 characters, and was formed in about 800 ce. At this time, other rune sets were or had been extended to 28 or more runes. However, rather than an increase in runes, the Younger Futhark had a reduced amount of runes, and some rune symbols were used to represent multiple sounds. Some runes even changed in meaning. The younger Futhark had several variations which evolved even further over the centuries.

The Younger Futhark was used well into the Middle Ages, particularly in Iceland were Christianity had less influence. However, the Roman alphabet was eventually preferred and use of the Younger Futhark was ultimately forbidden.

Self-Styled Modern Rune Rows

There are additional self-styled modern rune rows to those listed below. I have chosen the most well known ones.

Armanen Runes and the Nazis

The Armanen runes (or Armanen Futharkh) were invented by Austrian born German nationalist Guido List, better known as Guido von List, an author, journalist, and occultist. There are 18 runes in the Armanen row, which resembles mostly the Younger

Futhark (of 16 runes) but with differences in some symbols and meanings. Von List claimed they were revealed to him in an "inner eye" vision during a period of temporary blindness after a cataract operation in 1902. These runes were the subject of his book *The Secrets of the Runes*. He said they were encrypted in stanzas 138 to 165 of the *Havamal* (from the *Poetic Edda*), although his claims remains unproven.

It is thought that it is these runes which found favor with various members of the Nazi party of which some were adopted as emblems; perhaps the best-known is the insignia of the SS, which is a double *Sowilo* (or *Sowelo*) symbol. It was known as *Sigil* to the Nazis.

It is not surprising then, that after the war the runes in general fell out of favor with the rest of the world. However, in the 1980s there was yet another revival, although Tolkien had already used them to good advantage in his books.

The Witch's Runes

"Witch's Runes" are commonly displayed in New-age shops and bookshops. You will also find them on the internet in occult sites. The Witch's Runes are an invention of Susan Sheppard in the late twentieth century. There are 13 runes in this set, and they are original in symbols and meanings. They are popular among modern witches. They are not to be confused with the original rune rows also popular with witches.

Theban Runes (Theban Alphabet)

These runes are sometimes called *Witches' Runes* and *Runes of Honorius*. This alphabet comes from Henry Cornelius Agrippa's *Third book of Occult Philosophy* first published in Antwerp in 1531. This alphabet is mainly used by Pagans, Witches and Wiccans, as a secret writing code and occasionally in magical talismans. It was brought to the attention of Wiccans by Gerald Gardner.

The Blank Rune

If you have bought your runes or have looked at advertisements for them, you will often find that they contain a "spare" rune which is blank. This is actually called the blank rune.

The blank rune is a modern addition made popular by the author Ralph Blum. He is said to have found it in a rune set he purchased. Believing it was significant, he then gave a meaning to it of his own creation. My guess is that it was included as a spare in case one was lost. As this is a modern addition and runes are read according to their signs and the hidden symbolic meanings behind them, I see no reason to include it at all. Accordingly, and at no offence meant to others, you will not find it included in this book.

What the Runes Can Do for Us

Runes are a tool for personal growth and transformation. They can help you in your everyday life and in your everyday decisions. When you cast the runes they will tap into your unconscious, they will talk to you, teach you, and guide you. They will help you to get to know the real you, the whole you.

You do not need to be actually psychic to read the runes. However, the runes will help you to develop your intuitive abilities. As you become familiar with them, the runes begin to communicate with you, and you will learn how to interpret them using your intuition in combination with the symbolism.

The runes work in a magical way. Each one has special properties that can help you in their own distinct manner. After a time, when you get to know the runes, you will feel which ones can help you personally. My favorite rune, one that I feel is connected to me, is *Uruz* the rune of strength and luck, another one is *Ehwaz*. For you it likely to be a different rune or runes that you come to feel a true affiliation with, a rune that perhaps helps you through testing times in your life.

To understand fully how this works, a personal connection to the runes is most desirable. To help develop this connection, then it is essential to first have an understanding of runelore.

Chapter 2

Runelore

What is Mythology?

To understand mythology, first we should acquire a feeling or passion for it as we would for a favorite interest such as poetry. The mystical meaning of mythology has been lost to us over the centuries as inhibiting scientific thought progressed, along with much of what connected us to Spirit, without and within. In ancient times, the minds of the people were uncontaminated with scientific thought, and they were much more guided by their natural instincts. We can only benefit by approaching myths with an open, uncluttered mind, as it will assist us in gaining a spiritual insight, which in turn helps us build a better connection with the runes.

In reading the myths, we should remember that in the past, mythology was not read about, it was lived. For those people this was their religion and they believed in it, just as we believe in our own histories and religions. Myths were not myths to the peoples of the past, but a mutable epic narrative they trusted in and lived by.

To many people, myths are tales invented by the uneducated, ignorant, and superstitious peoples of ancient times. Moreover, myths are now often analyzed for historical, linguistic, and psychological meanings or interpretations, by people who have perhaps not taken pleasure in them simply for what they are, and more often than not, approach their analysis with what can only be described as a dull rationality. Of course there is always the exception. It is not that some of these interpretations are not useful when it comes to connecting them with the discovery of the Self. But if we look at poetry for instance, when it is analyzed too much, it takes away the pure enjoyment of it and the experience of just letting the poetry speak for itself. We should therefore, in connecting mythology with the runes, learn to see it as a lived philosophy, and put the soul back into it.

The Runes and Mythology

Mythology is very important when studying the runes, to understand the mystical and magical aspects of them. The runes came from mythology and studying them in that context helps us gain an all-important spiritual connection. According to myth, the chief Norse god Odin, found the runes when he hung upside down in a self-sacrificing ritual, on what is generally believed to be Yggdrasil, the Norse World Tree. He hung there for nine days and nine nights, without food or water and impaled on a spear. Finding the runes on the ground, he took them up.

This story of how Odin found the runes is told in the poem, The *Havamal* (Words of the High One). The *Havamal* is part of the *Poetic Edda*.

139. I ween that I hung | on the windy tree,
Hung there for nights full nine;
With the spear I was wounded, | and offered I was
To Othin, myself to myself,
On the tree that none | may ever know
What root beneath it runs.

140. None made me happy | with loaf or horn,
And there below I looked;
I took up the runes, | shrieking I took them,
And forthwith back I fell.

141. Nine mighty songs | I got from the son
Of Bolthorn, Bestla's father;

And a drink I got | of the goodly mead
Poured out from Othrörir.

142. Then began I to thrive, | and wisdom to get,
I grew and well I was;
Each word led me on | to another word,
Each deed to another deed.

143. Runes shalt thou find, | and fateful signs,
That the king of singers colored,
And the mighty gods have made; Full strong the signs, | full mighty
the signs
That the ruler of gods doth write.

144. Othin for the gods, | Dain for the elves,
And Dvalin for the dwarfs,
Alsvith for giants | and all mankind,
And some myself I wrote.

145. Knowest how one shall write, | knowest how one shall rede?
Knowest how one shall tint, | knowest how one makes trial?
Knowest how one shall ask, | knowest how one shall offer?
Knowest how one shall send, | knowest how one shall sacrifice?

146. Better no prayer | than too big an offering,
By thy getting measure thy gift;
Better is none | than too big a sacrifice,
.   .   .   .
So Thund of old wrote | ere man's race began,
Where he rose on high | when home he came.
Translated by Henry Adams Bellows

In this poem Odin speaks of the elves, dwarfs, and giants. These
beings can be found residing in the realms of the World Tree,

Yggdrasil. Odin says that many people took part in making the runes, and some he carved himself. So you can see how the runes relate to mythology already.

Let us look in more detail at some of the lines of the *Havamal* and decide what this means to us in modern times. These lines have slightly different meanings depending on which translation is used.

The first two lines: *Knowest how one shall write,* | *knowest how one shall rede?* These lines concern the carving or scoring of the runes and knowing them well. Scoring can be seen as a magical act and like all of the standards lain down in the Havamal, is required if we want to learn the runes.

The second two lines: *Knowest how one shall tint,* | *knowest how one makes trial?* These lines concern the staining of the symbols onto the runes, and how they should be checked ready for use. It is important to know how by staining, you put something into them from yourself, and therefore make a connection. You also need to know what you are doing. You need to be familiar with the runes themselves.

The third two lines: *Knowest how one shall ask,* | *knowest how one shall offer?* These lines could concern the asking for spiritual help (evocation) in interpreting of the runes before casting, and offering something in exchange. In modern times this perhaps means leaving a gift such as burning incense or offering flowers. Alternatively, this could equally mean empowering and making a spiritual link with Deity.

The fourth two lines: *Knowest how one shall send,* | *knowest how one shall sacrifice?* These final lines concern the sending out of the power of the spell when using them for magic and "spending" or dissipating the spell when it has served its purpose, or perhaps neutralizing an inappropriate charm. The sacrifice or offering here probably refers to Odin's sacrifice he made in order to gain the runes and receive enlightenment. We sacrifice our time to learn the runes.

We have to work hard by following the above process to gain knowledge of the runes and achieve a spiritual bond. And this is perhaps why it is a good idea to make our own runes if we are able. However, if we are using stones or crystals that are too hard to score (carve), then we will have to leave this out, but it is useful to keep to the spirit of this process as far as possible.

The above lines are also appropriate to rune magic and you can read about this in Chapter 8.

The Eddas

The *Poetic Edda* is a collection of 34 Old Norse poems of the late thirteenth century although probably composed earlier (possibly 800-1200 CE), and most likely in Iceland although possibly in Norway. The *Poetic Edda* along with the *Prose Edda* is a primary written source of Norse Mythology. The author is unknown. The *Poetic Edda* narrates the creation myths and also myths about the individual gods. The second part recounts the legends of other heroes and heroines.

The *Prose Edda* also known as the *Younger Edda*, contains stories from Norse Mythology, and is attributed to Icelandic historian, Snorri Sturluson and written around 1222. It was written as guide to skaldic poetry (poems of the song-smiths). The first two parts are concerned with mythological stories, the third is a delivery of skaldic poetry, and the last part is a discussion on the meters of the poems.

The Rune Poems

There are several rune poems in existence that provide the meanings of the runes. None are very ancient but come from the centuries ce. The poems were probably written to aid in memorizing and for the passing on of the lore to others. The rune poems are vital to those studying the runes, not just for divination and magic, but also for historical research.

There are four surviving rune poems which list the runes and their meanings. These give the meanings of the runes as we now know them. One is known as the *Abecedarium Nordmanicum* written down in the ninth century CE, although there is some dispute whether it can be classed as a poem.

The other three rune poems and those most often used are the *Old Icelandic*, the *Old Norwegian* and the *Old English Rune Poems*.

The *Old Norwegian Rune Poem*, is from around the twelve to thirteenth century CE, and has much in the way of Christian influences.

The *Old Icelandic Rune Poem* is the most recent, dating from the fifteenth century CE.

The *Old English Rune Poem* is the oldest of these. Again dates are approximate of when it was written but it is thought to be between the eighth and tenth centuries CE. This is the only poem that covers all 24 of the runes in the Elder Futhark, and the one which we are going to study. However, it does accompany the Anglo-Saxon/Anglo-Frisian rune row, so it contains 29 verses to accommodate all the runes of that row, but I have only included the 24 verses that pertain to the Elder Futhark. Below is my modernized version of the rune poem to make it easier to understand.

The Old English Rune Poem
Money is a comfort to everyone.
Though every man should deal it out freely,
if he wants approval from the Lord.

The aurochs (wild ox) is savage. A fierce beast,
it fights with its great horns. A well known
wanderer of the moors, it has a courageous spirit.

The thorn is very sharp, for every thane,
who grasps at it. It is harmful and will cause pain,
to every man that rests on it.

The mouth is the source of all speech.
It is the support of wisdom, and the wise man's counsel.
And to the noble warrior it is inspiration and happiness.

Riding is in the hall, to every warrior easy.
But mighty hard for those who sit on a strong horse,
Over miles of roads.

The torch is to the living, known by its flame.
Shining bright, it burns most often,
where the nobles rest, inside the hall.

A gift to every man is gaiety and praise,
support and worthiness. And to every outcast,
honor and nourishment, when they would otherwise have nothing.

Joy is enjoyed by those who know little of need,
pain, and sorrow. Who is blessed with prosperity,
and is content with his house.

Hail is the whitest of grains.
It whirls from the heavens,
and tossed by gusts of wind, it turns to water.

Need constricts the chest,
though to children of men it often brings,
help and healing, if heeded in time.

Ice is very cold and vastly slippery.
It glistens like glass, or a jewel,
The ground formed of frost, is a fair to behold.

The harvest brings hope to man,
If God lets the earth, bestow her bright

fruits on both the rich and the needy.

The yew is outwardly a rough tree.
Held hard and fast in the earth, it is the guardian of fire.
Deeply rooted, it is a joy on the estate.

Gaming is always play and laughter,
among bold men and where warriors sit,
in the beer hall in merriment together.

The elk sedge grows most often in the marsh,
It waxes in water, and grimly wounds
And makes red with blood, any man who dares to grasp it.

The sun is by seamen, always hoped for,
When they sail over the fishes' bath,
Until the sea horse, they bring to land.

Tir is a sign that holds loyalty well,
with the nobles; on its straight course,
over night's mists, it is unfailing.

The birch is fruitless, still it bears
twigs without fertile seed, its shining branches
high on its crown loaded with leaves, reach to the sky.

The horse before earls, a noble's pleasure.
Proud on its hooves, around it wealthy heroes
exchange speech. Ever a comfort to the restless.

Man in his joy, is dear to his kinsmen,
Though each shall have to part from the other,
when by the Lord's judgment he is entrusted to the earth.

Water is to folk thought endless when they sail forth
on an unstable ship. The great waves of the sea terrify,
And the seahorse heeds not the bridle.

Ing was first seen among the East Danes, until
eastward he went over the waves, with his wagon,
And thus the warriors named the hero.

Day is the Lord's messenger, dear to man,
The leaders great light, a joy and hope
to rich and poor, is a benefit to all.

The estate is dear to every man.
If he can take pleasure in what he has,
More often will prosper.

The verses give good insight into the meanings of each of the
runes though it does not name them. Although they relate to the
Anglo Saxon/Anglo Frisian runes, if we look at the last two
verses, which start with "Day" and "Estate" we can see that they
also relate to the last two runes of the Elder Futhark. *Dagaz*
means "day" and *Othala* means "estate" or "homestead". There is
a corresponding verse for each of the runes and by reading them
you will begin to seek out your own definitions and come to your
own conclusions concerning the meanings. To help you, when we
look at my own interpretation of the rune meanings we will look
at the verses in this poem in more detail.

Mythological Main Points

I cannot write here everything there is to learn about Norse
mythology without copying and interpreting the Eddas, or
rewriting a whole wealth of myths. So I will write a little about
the main points from which to start and leave you to read the
myths in your own time. At the end of the book you can read

more about the chief Norse gods and goddesses of the Northern Pantheon.

The Creation Myth

In the beginning there was a yawning great void. And the void was called Ginnungagap. The first land to exist was Muspelheim, a place of fire and great heat. And there was Niflheim, the dark land of fog and ice.

When the warm air met the cold, the ice began to melt and from the drops of the thaw grew the primeval giant Ymir. While Ymir slept he sweated, and from this under his left arm grew a man and a woman and his legs produced a son, and this was the beginning of the frost giants. Next from the thawing frost came Audhumla the cow. Rivers of milk came from her teats and from this she nourished Ymir.

Audhumla incessantly licked at the salty ice with her warm tongue. After a day of licking a man's hair came into view, and after two days his head appeared, and after the third day the whole man was freed. His name was Buri. Buri had a son named Bor and Bor married Bestla the daughter of a giant.

Bor and Bestla had three sons, the first was Odin and he was the greatest and the most noble, the second son was Vili, and the third was Ve.

Odin and his brothers killed Ymir, and from his wounds the flowing blood drowned all the frost giants, except for one, and that was Bergelmir. He escaped with his wife and produced another race of frost giants in the land of Jotunheim.

The three brothers then took the body of Ymir and made the world from his body. From his blood came the sea and lakes, from his flesh the earth, from his hair the trees, from his teeth they made the rocks and pebbles, and from his broken bones came the mountains.

They then moved onto the sky and night sky. From Ymir's skull, the brothers fashioned the sky, and placed it over the earth and under the four corners of the sky they placed dwarfs named, Nordi, Sudri, Austri and Vestri (North, South, East and West). They flung Ymir's brains into the sky to become the clouds, and used the sparks of the still burning fires

*of Muspelheim to light the earth from above in the form of the sun, moon
and stars.*

*While walking along the sea shore the three brothers found two tree
trunks, and from these they created man and woman. It was Odin who
breathed life and spirit into them, and Vili who gave them understanding and emotion, and lastly Ve gave them the abilities of sight,
hearing, and speech. The man was named Ask (from the Ash tree) and
the woman Embla (the elm tree). From Ask and Embla sprang all the
races of humankind.*

*The brothers built for themselves in the heavens a land called
Asgard. The Aesir gods and their families settled there. For humankind
they built the land of Midgard. To link the two, the gods built a bridge
linking heaven to earth, and this was called Bifrost the Rainbow Bridge
and it was guarded by Heimdall. However, at Ragnarok Bifrost will
break when the giants ride over it.*

The Norns

Urd, Verdandi, and Skuld, are known as The Norns, and they are
often said to be a Norse triple goddess rather like the Greek
goddesses "The Fates" in that they are the weavers of the tapestry
of fate. The Norns were called the "Weirdes" (various spellings)
by Chaucer in *The Legend of Good Women* and *Troilus and Criseyde*,
and the "Weird Sisters" by Shakespeare as the three witches in his
play *Macbeth*.

The Norns live beneath Yggdrasil. They take water from the
Well of Urd (fate), and with the clay or sand that lies around it,
pour it over the branches of Yggdrasil to save them from decay.
They control the destinies of both gods and men as well as the
unchanging laws of the cosmos.

They are represented as three sisters: Urd (the past or that
which has become), Verdandi (the present, or that which is
becoming) and Skuld (the future or that which will be). Perhaps
the most noteworthy of the Norns is Urd, as she is associated with
wyrd and with *orlog* too. However, as a triple goddess we can

view the Norns as a single force, and therefore their three characteristics as interrelated (as indicated in the explanation of *Orlog and Wyrd* below).

You can call on The Norns as Spiritual Guides to help you in interpreting your readings.

Orlog and Wyrd

Orlog and *wyrd* are both vital in understanding Norse cosmology and the interpreting of the runes, and as they are closely connected I am going to explain them together. However, attempting to make head or tale of both concepts is as tricky as trying to sort out the threads of the web of wyrd itself. There are so many definitions and one person has a different perspective on it than the next. Some people say they have the same meaning of *fate*. Below is my own, I believe plausible explanation, and you may agree or otherwise.

Orlog can be defined as "primal law" (and is written similar to the Dutch word "oorlog", meaning war and possibly has similar origins), and it exists within and through all creation. No one escapes this law as it is the destiny of man and gods alike, and is something which we cannot manipulate. Perhaps it can be best explained as a continuous succession of causes and effects that determined our past actions and the consequences of them, and which endures throughout our lives. These past actions create the future. Accordingly, it is *that which has become* but is linked with *that which is becoming* and *that which will be*.

However, although past actions cannot be altered, we can work on the way we behave to change aspects of repeated negative behavior and in doing so we weave the *web of wyrd*. So in this way, one researcher will state that orlog is immutable and some that it is transformed by present and future actions. If in the future we look back to our past actions from now onwards, we might indeed find that in the meantime, in changing the way we behaved (working on our wyrd), that the patterns of our orlog have indeed changed. But still, we cannot again change those actions, good or bad, that have already happened. And those actions affect our overall fate.

So then are we born with orlog or not? Well, the circumstances of our births do affect our lives by at least placing limitations on us, which can be difficult to dislodge. If we are a first-born son or daughter of a king and heir to the throne, our destiny will be that one day we will be king or queen unless we abdicate or stand down (presuming we did not die in the meantime). However, our lives are still affected by our birth circumstances as we are still, in the chain of continuous cause and effect, at the mercy of our orlog. Even though we stood down to change the order of what life was attempting to impose upon us, we will always be son or daughter of a king, and there will still be the consequences of this action to face. How we handle those consequences adds threads to web of our wyrd.

The same applies if we were born within an extremely poor family in a country that often suffers famine, which possibly means we are destined for a life of suffering of varying degrees, unless or until we find a way of escape. Even we do escape our birth circumstances will affect the way we behave in the future.

Therefore, the lives of our predecessors do help to create our orlog, and we cannot change the circumstances of this. Ultimately though, we still have responsibility for how we conduct ourselves and the choices we make in life.

To make this easier I have put this into an example. Let us say we have done or said something wrong. Well, we cannot stop the consequences of this as it is already done, as no one can avoid the law of orlog. However, we have two choices now in the present, and that is either to leave things as they are and accept the fallout, or go and at least attempt to put everything right. Either choice will affect the future, even though we cannot escape the past. And in making our choice we are again weaving the web of our personal wyrd.

Wyrd relates to orlog. The word *weird* derives from it, though it is not how we understand it in modern times.

Wyrd influences us as an individual, but we are also influenced by the continual restrictions caused by the collective wyrd of our ancestry and community (or universal wyrd). So, while we are constrained by orlog, or fixed past actions and their past, present and future consequences, we create our own wyrd by how we react to those past actions in our present situation, and they in turn are woven into the web. We build up layer upon layer of past actions and reactions. However, it is not just the layers of our own actions, but also those of others whose actions have affected us and will continue to do so. For instance if our husband or wife walks out on us, it will affect our future, and in turn the future of any children in the relationship. So in fact, all actions are interconnected and this is what is called the web of wyrd.

We all have strengths and weaknesses. These aspects of our personality, or our personal wyrd, will lead us through life. Working against our wyrd can cause trials and tribulations. We cannot or perhaps should not change who we essentially are, perhaps by sacrificing our principles or going against our morals, as doing this can only lead to personal trauma, and cause a tangle in our web. So it is better to learn to live and work with our wyrd.

The threads of the web of wyrd are continual, like the web of the spider. We cannot escape it as we are caught up in it, but perhaps we can alter future patterns in a positive way. For example we can endeavor to learn to accept the strengths of our anima/animus, and the weaknesses of our shadow (explained in the *Glossary of the Psyche* at the end of the book), and then to use them to our best advantage. In the same way, we can attempt to accept and use our individual wyrd, though it will be challenging. And by doing so we are able in some way to at least influence the weaving of fate.

An example here would be for instance a woman who cannot learn to say "no" because she feels obliged to say "yes" and this can be for many different reasons. In this scenario the woman is certain she wants to change, so she can gain more freedom for herself.

Well, here she gains the power to alter this pattern by plucking up the courage to say "no" instead of "yes" because she has never had the chance to form her own relationship as she is always so busy doing things for others. She learns to refuse to let herself be used as the family babysitter, or be coerced into doing extra shifts at work for those who ask. She cannot do this suddenly, but she gradually introduces it by saying she already has commitments she cannot get out of, but might be available next week though. Little by little she adds to it until she is no longer available at the drop of a hat. After a time the other people find alternative arrangements because they could no longer presume that this woman would be the one to do it (and perhaps deep down knew they were taking advantage of her). The woman continues to help people but on her own terms as she does not want to alter who she really is.

During this time the woman looks at her own past and examines her wyrd to see why she became stuck in this pattern of behavior in the first place. Perhaps it was because she worried how people would view her, and learnt to (wrongly) accept that this must be her destiny. But it could possibly have been because she formed the pattern in childhood, as she was a timid child with dominant siblings and was afraid to stand up to them. Or perhaps it was an ego or self-image problem, in that she actually liked to be thought of as indispensable, or worse still, enjoyed being a martyr. By confronting her past behavior, and although not being able to go back in time to behave differently, she can at least to some extent influence the future patterns of her wyrd.

So what has this to do with the runes? When we cast the runes we usually ask a question about a problem or dilemma. Through casting the runes, the runecaster attempts to get to the root of the problem or *that which has become*. So to clarify, when we have a problem, and we want to know in a rune casting what the outcome will be, we look at the present state of our own or someone else's *wyrd*. We can see by the runes we choose, what in the past is affecting the present and the future. So in fact, we analyze the web of wyrd and in doing so, we can perhaps discover those hidden truths which will give us an insight into the problem. We can then influence the possible outcomes that have been revealed. It might be in a way that can only lessen the impact of the consequences of past actions, as we cannot manipulate orlog, but we can alter to our advantage the patterns of the present and future. In this way the past is fixed, the present is in constant change, and the future is still to be determined (but yet transformable).

If we can learn to recognize and accept *synchronistic* events (Chapter 5), then it will help us in recognizing those same hidden truths, which will in turn assist us in unraveling the threads of the web of wyrd, and it will also help us in making a personal connection to the runes.

Chapter 3

The Connection

Seeing the Wind

Look and you will see
the invisible wind.
Reach out and you will grasp
the ungraspable air.
Everything is possible
for seekers of the unreachable.
Voyage
beyond the beyond,
the hidden you will find. There,
in the fathomless places
of the mind.

I was once taking part in a poetry exercise. We were given a poem to read and then we had to guess the age and sex of the writer. Some students said young and female, another said thirties and male, and my own choice was menopausal age and female. Everyone saw something different. The poem had different meanings for all of us over and beyond the words written. As so it is with the runes. The runes like the poem, speak directly to us. There is the basic meaning, and then there is the secret meaning accessed through the interaction of mind, matter and spirit; for the runes reveal both inner and outer truths. This magical symbolic language is used to communicate between man and God or microcosm and macrocosm, and the conscious and the unconscious. We will call these the spiritual and psychic connections, which will combine to become a personal connection.

The Spiritual Connection

One thing our ancestors surely had over us was a distinct spiritual connection with the runes. Because of their beliefs, they were able to trust in the magic of them. They could call on a higher power to help make that connection in a way that is more difficult now. If you do not believe in the power of the Norse gods and goddesses of mythology, then there is no point in invoking or evoking them to help you with your readings. Yet, perhaps this will cause you to feel that in not doing so you cannot connect as fully as others might do, and as a result would like an alternative. In that case I would like to suggest other options such as the ancient ancestors, nature, Spirit Guides, faery folk or elementals. Whichever you choose, it will be better if you can link your choice of a higher or magical power with the Northern Mysteries for in doing so you will be preserving the all important spirit of the runes.

Some people embarking on rune study will question if they even have to call on a higher spiritual power. Do the runes work as well without it? That is something you need to discover for yourself. But to make a complete connection with the runes is to use them to their full potential.

The Psychic Connection

To gain a psychic connection we need to learn to "look". Years of denial, fear of the unknown, and lack of using certain areas of our brains and psyche has diminished our ability to see things that we otherwise could have access to. We need to use our "third eye" and learn to look and see what up to now has been invisible to us.

Everyone has psychic abilities, but not everyone uses them. This leads to varying levels of psychic skills. Many people call clairvoyance a gift and it is to the people who do not have to try so hard to achieve results. The rest of us have to put more effort in.

Some psychic people have relatives who also have heightened psychic awareness, perhaps in different ways, so it can be hereditary. In addition, we all have varying levels of psychic maturity. As children, we are often more psychic than in young adulthood, fear or ridicule causes us to hide or dismiss our skills. But by confronting our fears at being ridiculed and looking weird, we can regain that lost ability.

To increase our intuitive abilities we need to practice using them with confidence regardless of our level of ability. The more we use our sixth sense, the better we will become. We have to learn to recognize our intuition and trust in it. Some people have intuitive dreams, others healing skills, some are prophetic, or have strong intuition, and others can communicate with spirits. All of us have experienced those strange feelings of déjà vu, or startling moments when we are thinking of someone and they call or phone, or sing a song and then switch the radio on to find that the same song is playing. Then there are synchronous moments, which you can read about in Chapter 5.

If you practice seeing auras, then you are already tuning into your sixth sense. If you progress to seeing them, then you are heightening your psychic awareness. Intuition has to be worked on, interpreted, and refined, and it then becomes more precise. You can learn more about this in the exercises below.

Divination is a good way of increasing psychic skills. Many psychics use divination as a catalyst to their insight. Divination helps us focus on matters in hand and separate insight from random thoughts. Without divination the psychic often has to "tune in" and this takes a little longer, but the end results are the same.

When we cast the runes as a non-psychic or with limited psychic abilities, we are calling on a hidden intuitiveness to help us to interpret the runes and in turn the runes help us with our everyday life problems and situations.

Psychic Exercises
Sometimes when we talk to people we know they are lying. This

is your intuition at work. Perhaps you have a friend who has a relationship problem that you have your own thoughts about. Do these thoughts keep repeating? Write down any strong impressions. Concentrate and focus on a matter, do you have any prominent thoughts? Again write them down. You can check later if you were right or at least on the right lines.

Regularly use the visualization exercises at the end of this chapter and Chapter 5, and write down your messages or thoughts.

Practice reading candles auras. You can do this by choosing a time when it is dusk or the room has limited lighting. Set up two or three different colored dinner candles. Stare at the candle and even when blinking, hold your gaze. Let your eyes go slightly out of focus. After a short time, you should be able to see an aura. Try it with the other candles and see if they have auras of other colors. If you do see the aura, what does the basic candle color signify to you?

This exercise will teach you to be more confident. Find a pack of playing cards and lay them out face down in rows. Keep a pen and paper handy. Before turning over each card, try to predict first its color, then if you are feeling particularly confident, the suit, and finally the number or picture. Record your findings on paper. If you only get a strong impression of color or suit, then only record those things. If you have no strong impressions, then work on your first thoughts. You will probably find that you will use a mixture of both, and that some cards will take you longer to focus on.

When practicing any of these exercises, try to do it when you are feeling alert and cannot be disturbed or distracted, as it will be difficult to keep your concentration.

And lastly, keep a dream diary. Record your dreams daily over one month. You are the best person to interpret your dreams as they are individual to you. Look carefully at your dream imagery. What do the people or places in the dream signify, or the animals or objects? Look at the dreams over the whole month and see if there is a connection. Your dreams originate in the unconscious and come into the conscious mind; possibly telling you things you need to know, revealing fears, or advising you. Sometimes they are surprisingly simple and perhaps prompted by a Television program or a book you are reading, and do not have any great significance. However, they should not be dismissed because they seem weird, chaotic, incoherent, or even down right ridiculous.

Visualization Exercise 1
Now before we go onto Chapter 4, it is time to make your first connection with the runes. Be prepared for startling results with this exercise. Persevere if this does not happen straight away. Visualizations Exercises 1 and 2 should be regularly practiced.

Read the visualization exercise below, to gain some idea of what you need to do first. Rather than describe everything for you, I hope to encourage you to look, see, and hear for yourself. Visualization is calming, magical, and teaches you to focus. The exercise can be altered somewhat to fit with your own thoughts and what will work best for you. For instance, you might prefer to visualize you are in a rainforest, close to the sea, or in a meadow, if this suits you better. All the preparations below for the exercise are to be repeated for Visualization Exercise 2 and 3 in Chapter 5.

What you will need
Purple candles
Meditation music
Your runes
Incense: Either make your own and burn it in a safe container on incense charcoal (available from New Age shops), or use incense sticks or cones of sandalwood and frankincense. If you are making your own mix together a selection of the following

available from New Age shops or the kitchen:

Frankincense

Sandalwood

Mugwort (can be found at the side of roads, wasteland, or natural meadows)

Wormwood

Jasmine

Dandelion

Bay

Cinnamon

If you find any of the above difficult to find then you can mix any of the above with any of the following:

Parsley

Lavender

Clove

Clover

Linden

Sage

Chamomile

Thyme

Catnip

Any of the herbs can be substituted for a few drops of essential oil.

Find yourself a quiet, private space, perhaps in your bedroom or even in a secluded garden. Light the candles, burn the incense, and play the music low.

However if you do not have the resources to buy these items, or the private space, do not despair, just do what you can to make a lovely calm peaceful spot, with perhaps a stick of incense, a candle or two, and some non-intrusive classical music played low.

You can sit or recline for this exercise. But make sure you have your bag of runes on your lap. The suggestions below as you walk thorough the forest in the visualization, are just that, suggestions. Look around you all the time and make a mental note of anything significant you see. Take your time as the exercise should last at least twenty minutes.

Once you are comfortable and settled take a few deep breaths and relax all of your body. Try to banish any thoughts that are not to do with the exercise from your mind. You can do this by closing your eyes, and imagining a tree and examining all the components of it. Now open your eyes, and take your bag of runes and with your power hand (the one you write with) feel around and choose a rune. Do *not* look at it; just hold it in your hand. Put the bag of runes aside.

Settle down again and close your eyes. Breathe slowly in and out. Feel the tenseness leave your muscles. If you have difficulty with this, start at your toes and then gradually relax all your muscles in your legs, hands, arms, and trunk and all the way up to your head. Lastly relax your face muscles.

Now, imagine yourself on a forest path, it is early summer. Hold the thought while you get your bearings. Then continue.

You are walking along a forest path. Sunlight filters through the green-leaved trees. The bracken among the trees is the color of jade. Beneath your feet are the remains of last autumn's russet leaves. The air is warm and a soft breeze gently ruffles your hair. The birds are singing their summer songs and you smell the wild flowers edging the path.

Ahead of you the path winds, but you do not see where it leads. In the distance you can hear trickling water, but you cannot see from where. Look around you, what can you see — a bird? What kind of bird? A deer, or a rabbit, or possibly something not even connected with creatures of nature. Perhaps you see a flower, a person, a spectacular tree, or a nature spirit. There might be a mist swirling through the trees.

What about your other senses? Can you hear anything apart from the water, bird calling, or an animal growling, or a fire crackling? What can you smell? Musty, old leaves or smoke might assault your nostrils, or the beautiful scent of the wild rose floats past you. Touch the bark of a tree, feel its roughness. Is the ground hard or soft?

You continue along the path feeling the rune in your hand. There is magic in the air. The path is widening in front of you and soon you meet the running water. It is a wide stream. The water is running faster and suddenly it drops down into a pretty waterfall. You decide to stop here. You follow the path downhill a little and you find yourself a big flat stone and sit down on it close to the waterfall. You watch as the blue damselflies dart back and forth over the water or a jeweled dragonfly whirs overhead.

You are again aware of the rune in your hand. Look around you. What can you see that is connected to the rune? Do you something simple, like a butterfly, bee, or flower, or something more significant like a tree, animal or person? Is it is a feeling, and is that feeling dark or negative, or bright and positive? Perhaps you see a cloud or it might rain, snow or hail. Possibly the sun comes out or a rainbow appears. Do not ignore any changes in scenery. No matter what you decide upon it is fine. Even if you think surely the small thing you have noticed cannot be the connection to the rune, if that is all you can see, it is perfectly alright. Now look awhile until you have decided on your symbol.

Now take two deep breaths, and very slowly open your eyes. You will feel disorientated so give yourself a few moments to recover. When you feel sufficiently recovered, look at the rune you have in your hand. What is it?

You will now see the object of the exercise. Concentrate on the rune symbol and see if the image (or images) in your head connects with it. You can then look up the meanings in Chapter 4. Does the rune mean anything personal to you? Do you see a direct link? Was it so accurate that it spooked you? Perhaps you even knew which rune you held. If you had none of these things, do not worry, just persevere and eventually you will see results. Some people will see good results almost every time, and others will take longer, it will all depend on your concentration and how far your psyche is developed. Even if the link appears a weak one, you are already on your way to making a connection with your runes. Try to do the exercise often.

If you have difficulty shutting out the rest of the world or keeping your focus, try this extra exercise. Go for a walk in nature. If you do not live close to countryside or a park, then walk around an area where there are trees, or look around your own garden or backyard if you have one. The trick is to look at everything around you without being distracted by your own thoughts.

Look upwards, what do you see? What color is the sky? Are there any clouds? What color are they? Can you see treetops? What do you see among the branches? What color are the birds? Do you recognize any of them? If you feel your thoughts drifting to mundane things or even worries, bring your focus back. What is closer to the ground, a variety of plants and flowers? Can you name any of them? What do you see among them, butterflies, bees, a frog? Keep your focus the whole time you are walking. Do this often and then when you are meditating or visualizing, you will find it easier.

Chapter 4

Rune Meanings

Introduction to the Runes of the Elder Futhark

The 24 runes are divided into "aetter". Each aett (or eight runes within the set), are named after a Norse god (or perhaps a goddess). There are many different spellings for each rune and I have only included the ones that I use. All the stanzas belong to the *Old English Rune Poem*. This poem was written in the centuries after the Elder Futhark came into use and has Christian influences. But I hope you will find as I have, much in the poem that is of use.

I do not give reversed or murk meanings to the runes. A murk rune is commonly known as one that is face down showing the blank side and the bright side is face up, reversed it is upside down. Runes thrown outside a cast are often counted as murk runes. Some runes are not reversible as they are the same either way up, such as *Ingwaz* and *Sowilo*.

The reason I do not give murk or reverse meanings is because for me each rune has both positive and negative forces already, though not in equal amounts, especially when read in conjunction with other runes. As for murk meanings, a blank side has no visible symbol so has no meaning unless turned over. This does not mean that you cannot use reverse or murk meanings if you wish or prefer. It is a personal choice and some runecasters do use them and some do not. The ones that do use them often do so in different ways. Some ignore runes that are showing the blank side, but use others as reversed if they are upside down. Others will use the murk side and look at the rune to see what it is, but ignore it if it is upside down. So there is some ambiguity.

When casting the runes, I throw them onto my casting cloth

and choose them one at a time without looking. As I place each rune down, I automatically turn it over or the right way up before interpreting and without thinking about it. When I am casting onto circles I have a meaning for the outer edge of the cloth so interpret the runes that fall there, again turning them over as required.

Another point I would like to make here is that rune meanings vary according to writers. I have read criticism that for instance the *Algiz* rune is used for protection (by people with psychic abilities) and that there is no actual evidence of it being used for this purpose. This tells me that some people are rather rigid in their views. Many people, from their personal experience of the runes, have found it to be protective, including respected authorities of runelore. I do not believe that we necessarily have to restrict ourselves to the very limited and fragmentary evidence that is available. One thing most people agree on is that the runes are magical and spiritual. They speak to you and if you tune in you can learn from them. You should open you mind to them, not restrict yourself to a few meanings that can be found scattered throughout mythological writings, many which have been Christianized and written centuries later. I feel this is not what the runes are about. People have written and extended the meanings of the runes from years of working closely with them. Again, see what works for you, for your own experiences might tell you something new.

For magical purposes I have added a color or colors for each rune. You can use these colors for accompanying, candles, crystals, ribbons, or even your clothes. These are NOT the colors of the runes themselves. (General color correspondences are listed at the end of this book). I have also added the element associated with each rune.

Learning the Runes — Exercises
To learn the rune names and symbols try this exercise. Write down

the runes of the first aett. Learn these first before moving on to the next aett and test yourself by writing down the names of the runes. Now test yourself again this time just drawing the symbols. Now do both.

To learn the meanings try these methods. It will seem a complicated way to go about it, but it is more effective than just reading them from this book.

Use Visualization Exercise 1 in Chapter 3 daily choosing runes randomly. Alternatively, either choose a rune randomly from the bag, or start with Fehu. Read the meaning. Now put it under you pillow and see what reactions it evokes. Sleep with it overnight. Did you dream anything that connected with the rune meaning? Keep a notebook handy to make notes. The next day keep the rune with you for the whole day, and then the next night choose another.

You can use both exercises together if you have time. Start with the visualization, and then put the same rune under your pillow. Repeat daily if you have time.

Frey's Aett

Frey (meaning Lord) is the god of fertility, sun, rain, and is the patron of the bountiful harvest and ruler of Alfheim the land of the light elves. He is the brother of Freyja, and son of Njord the sea god. He is a god of the Vanir but joined the gods of the Aesir when the two realms were reconciled and Njord entered Asgard as part of an exchange. Frey's wife is the giantess Gerd, and he gave away his magic sword to his servant as a reward for helping him win her love. This will prove to be his downfall.

Freyja (meaning Lady) is the goddess of fertility, sensuality, love, beauty, music and childbirth. She is sister to Frey and daughter of Njord. She is famed for her beauty and her counterparts are Venus and Aphrodite in the Roman and Greek myths respectively. She is also said to be a sorceress as she is skilled in magic, especially *seidhr* magic. Freyja is young and full of life. She is fertile and ripe for pregnancy. Although filled with love and energy, she is also the battle goddess with much strength.

In Frey's Aett there are many brighter runes. This is the aett of enjoyment of life. You can expect much in the way of good fortune and success, new starts, new ventures, new friendships, and changes around the corner. You also have the strength to carry ventures through and to conquer obstacles along the way.

Fehu
Cattle — F
Element: Fire/Earth
Money is a comfort to everyone.
Though every man should deal it out freely,
if he wants approval from the Lord.

If we look at this stanza of the rune poem, we read that although it is all right to want or need money (as we all do), we should not keep it to ourselves if we want to prosper.

Cattle were used as currency in ancient times. Cattle symbolize protection, sheltering, and nourishment. If you had cattle, you had wealth and abundance. It was hard work looking after cattle, keeping them well fed, healthy and breeding from them. So it is earned wealth we are talking about here. The cattle did not magically appear like winning the lottery, although of course they could be inherited or gifted. It is also a wealth to be shared if you want to be looked favorably upon by the Divine.

Fehu is the rune of Frey who is of the Vanir gods of nature and is therefore also commonly associated with abundance and fertility. The cow is a fertile and domesticated animal and a symbol of Mother Earth. Audhumla the cow of the Norse Creation

Myth licked the salty ice uncovering a man Bor who became the father of Odin. *Fehu* can be called upon for use in fertility charms.

Fehu in a reading

Fehu can mean wealth and possessions won or earned. You have the strength to hold onto money, as long as you are prepared to use it wisely. Share your good fortune and avoid greed and self-indulgence. This is a transferable wealth and a good time for ventures or investments. If life is going well with you right now, persevere with any plans already made, and you will prosper. Luck is with you as this is a rune of general good fortune. *Fehu* indicates a fertile time, a time ripe for new beginnings of all kinds.

Keywords: Wealth, possessions, good fortune, prosperity, sharing, luck, fertility.

Counsel: Avoid greed and self-indulgence.

Colors: The accompanying colors I have assigned to *Fehu* are green and gold. Green and gold are traditional colors of money and wealth. Gold is also for luck and attraction. Green is also for Freyja, fertility, love and abundance. For magical purposes use one or both colors.

Uruz

Auroch — U

The aurochs (wild ox) is savage. A fierce beast,
it fights with its great horns. A well known wanderer
of the moors, it has a courageous spirit.

Element: Earth

If we look at the individual words of this stanza, the ones that stand out are "savage", "fierce", "great horns", "fights" and "courageous spirit". The aurochs is not afraid to walk the moors and meet with adversaries. He fights head on with them. He symbolizes masculine courage in battle.

The aurochs was a massive, powerful, but now extinct wild ox. It often reached more than two meters (six and a half feet) high at the shoulder and has sharp, curving horns. It was tenacious, courageous, strong, and was an animal to respect yet fear. The aurochs freely roamed the moors, independent and bold.

Uruz in a reading

Uruz is a masculine rune bringing you inner and outer strength. It is a little wild so try to keep it under control. It will help you battle adversity or to face challenges ahead. It shows stamina, fortitude, energy and passion. *Uruz* is sometimes compared to a horseshoe which is hung on doors for luck and it is considered a lucky rune. But strength is significant because being brave can bring you rewards.

You are protected. Creative ideas abound. This is a time of good health, general good luck and happiness. This is a rune for overcoming weaknesses and providing courage. This rune can signify raw masculine sexuality.

Keywords: Strength, stamina, energy, fortitude, tenacity, independence, passion, luck, creativity, courage, good health, happiness.

Counsel: Keep wildness under control.

Colors: The accompanying colors I have assigned to *Uruz* are orange and red, or an orange tinged red. Red is for vitality energy, courage and motivation. Orange is for strength, energy, and confidence. Use whichever color fits the best with your charm or spell.

Thurisaz
Giant or Thorn — TH
Element: Fire
The thorn is very sharp, for every thane,
who grasps at it. It is harmful and will cause pain,
to every man that rests on it.

In this stanza we read that the thorn is very sharp for every thane if he grabs at it (a thane is a man who perhaps gave military service in exchange for land and ranked above a freeman and below a nobleman in Anglo-Saxon England). Thorns are also harmful and will cause pain for those who rest on them. So we need to be wary.

Imagine a hedge of thorn protecting a property. It makes us safer from intruders, or it protects our plants and garden. It is also hard to penetrate, but impossible to penetrate safely. We can get through it, but not without some effort or perhaps injury. A good comparison here is with *Sleeping Beauty* from the fairy tale of the same name. She is protected against the wrong suitors, and only the right one can wake her up with a kiss. However, she is also imprisoned for a hundred years. No one can penetrate the thorns without facing certain death. Still the outcome is good as a prince braves the hedge of thorns and it disappears. She is discovered, kissed, and released from her curse.

Thurisaz in a reading
Thurisaz is the thorn or *thurs* meaning giant. It is connected with the god Thor, the giant slayer. This "thorny" rune does have a bad reputation unless it is in a positive cast. That is if the other runes around it are positive. The meaning then is not so severe.

With *Thurisaz*, on the one hand it can be protective but on the other difficulties can be expected as it symbolizes the forces of nature, tribulation, and adversity. But it is a rune which expects survival of those difficulties perhaps through self-assertion or use of wisdom.

Sometimes things have to get worse before they get better. You have to get rid of some aspects of your life to be able to move on. *Thurisaz* can be used for your protection if you need it, as hostile forces are at work. There is a period of difficulty ahead. Healthwise it can mean "women's problems". *Thurisaz* also has sexual connotations. Lust can be the negative force here. *Thurisaz* can be used as a rune of protection and carried or worn if negative energies are attacking you.

Keywords: Protective, forces of nature, tribulation, adversity, survival of difficulties, self-assertion.

Counsel: Lust can be a negative force.

Colors: The accompanying colors I have assigned to *Thurisaz* are red and black. Red is for survival, sexuality, potency and courage. Black is for its protective qualities. Use both or whichever rune is best suited to your charm or spell.

Ansuz
Mouth of Odin — A
Element: Air
The mouth is the source of all speech.
It is the support of wisdom, and the wise man's counsel.
And to the noble warrior it is inspiration and happiness.

This stanza tells us that *Ansuz* is the original source of all speech. Wisdom supports us and a wise man helps us. It is also inspiration and happiness, which has connotations of contentment.

The mouth of Odin is about communication and wisdom. The mouth is the organ of speech and breath of life, power of Spirit, and inspiration of the soul. It is the rune of Odin himself; he who gained enlightenment and knowledge of the runes.

Ansuz in a reading

When this rune comes up in a reading it shows that you have the power of communication, but use it wisely. This could be with talking to people, or writing emails or letters, or speaking on the telephone. It might even be your inner voice communicating with you, so use your intuition. In fact it is any form of communication.

It can also be teaching and listening. It is the creative rune of the poet and I also call it the "writing" rune. Good communication or advice may come from a wise man or mentor. If you are taking exams at the moment it means good luck in them.

You have the power of persuasion. If you need to negotiate with someone, then now is a good time to do it. As it provides inspiration, it is a good time to make changes in your life. General contentment is yours.

Keywords: Communication, wisdom, life-breath, inner voice, teaching, inspiration, persuasion, contentment.

Counsel: Use your power wisely.

Color: The accompanying color I have assigned to *Ansuz* is blue. Blue is for communication, wisdom, and intuition.

Raidho
Riding — R
Element: Air

Riding is in the hall, to every warrior easy.
But mighty hard for those who sit on a strong horse,
Over miles of roads.

In this stanza we read that for every warrior in the hall discussing it, the ride is easy. But it is mighty difficult for him who actually takes the long journey, even though he sits on a strong horse. Still of course, the warriors discuss it as an adventure.

When riding we have movement, a journey, excitement, pleasure and hard work. If we stay firm in the saddle we will progress forward. Riding makes us bold, venturing out into the wide world.

Raidho in a reading

Raidho often means a journey. This could be an actual journey to another country or possibly that you are about to embark on a spiritual journey, or another type of journey such as a university course of many years. It can also be a quest. Plan and be prepared. However, planning is the easy part because a long journey can sometimes be a difficult one that is tiring.

Raidho is also means of transportation so it could refer to a horse, bicycle, train, car, or airplane. It can mean the wish for change or the need for change.

The world is open to you, so move out of the boundaries of your comfort zone. Such boundaries can create a tenuous sense of security. Take a wider and less rigid view, and best of all look for new experiences. With *Raidho* you can be assured of movement as nothing stays still.

Keywords: Journey, excitement, pleasure, adventure, transportation, change, movement, new experiences.

Counsel: Move out of your comfort zone and venture out.

Color: The accompanying color I have assigned to *Raidho* is red. Red is for vitality, courage, power, and motivation.

Kenaz
Torch — K
Element: Fire
The torch is to the living, known by its flame.
Shining bright, it burns most often,
where the nobles rest, inside the hall.

This stanza tells of all of the living knowing the torch, and the power of the fire that burns shining and bright where the people rest. It tells us that indoors in a safe environment the torch shines bright, illuminating and cleansing. However, this implies that outside that safe environment, the fire will not be so controlled.

Kenaz the torch is a fire rune, and fire is creative, powerful, fertile, and illuminative but it is also destructive. It can be light or lightening. Fire is defensive and its light will guide us. Where the nobles rest is the hearth fire which is always kept burning to drive out evil.

Kenaz in a reading
In creative ventures it will lead the way, slowly but surely. And although nothing is going to be straightforward with this rune, as a torch it does illuminate a pathway for you. There is indeed a light at the end of the tunnel, just as spring follows winter.

Fire is protective and can ward off evil. But beware as it can also burn you. It can be good or bad depending on how it is used. Sometimes it is out of your control as fire has a will of its own. The forces of *Kenaz* are strong. It can denote heightened sexual passions, and in personal relationships it is wise to exercise caution.

Kenaz is a rune that is more difficult to understand so perseverance is necessary. When interpreting this rune it is wise to consider it more profoundly, and strongly use your intuition. What was the question asked? Does it concern the past, present or future? How is it in relation to other runes around it? Were you looking for guidance or was something or someone working against you? In time you will come to understand it better.

Keywords: Creative ventures, illumination, heightened sexual passion.

Counsel: Fire burns; keep it in control.

Colors: The accompanying colors I have assigned to *Kenaz* are red and orange. Red is for fire, power, passion, and sexuality. Orange is for creativity. For magical purposes use both colors.

Gebo
Gift — G
Element: Air

A gift to every man is gaiety and praise,
support and worthiness. And to every outcast,
honor and nourishment, when they would otherwise have nothing.

In this stanza we read that everyone has need of a gift. A gift brings happiness, praise, and support to the worthy. But even to the undeserving who would otherwise have nothing, it brings honor and nourishment.

Gebo is about giving and receiving. We give and people give back to us without us realizing it. We do a favor for someone and they do not forget it and do us a favor in return. These are gifts or exchanges. We need to watch out though for in the *Poetic Edda* it says: *It is better not to offer than to offer too much for a gift demands a gift.*

Gebo in a reading

Gebo often means an exchange of wedding rings, promises, or even kisses. It signifies happiness in a relationship. But beware of how many gifts you give or receive from someone as something is often expected back, or you will unconsciously expect something in return. In addition, gifts given in excess come to mean nothing. If you give without expecting anything in return, it is nourishment for the spirit.

You can be assured that with *Gebo* you can expect help or a gift from someone in the near future, and sometimes we all need gifts. This may come in the form of support.

Keywords: Gift, happiness, praise, support, honor, nourishment.

Counsel: Do not give or receive in excess.

Colors: The accompanying colors I have assigned to *Gebo* are green, blue, and gold. Green and gold are for abundance, good luck, and inner strength. Blue is for empathy, harmony, honesty and wisdom. Use green, or gold and blue for charms and spells.

Wunjo
Joy — W
Element: Earth
Joy is enjoyed by those who know little of need,
pain, and sorrow. Who is blessed with prosperity,
and is content with his house.

This stanza suggests that joy comes to those who are positive, and does not dwell on their pain and sorrows. If we are satisfied with what we have, then we will prosper in our lives.

Joy is happiness, pleasure and harmony. When we have joy, everything else appears to go well. We form positive thoughts and they attract even more joy. When we are happy we suffer less ill health. Joy and happiness are food for the soul.

Wunjo in a reading

With *Wunjo* everything is going well. It means happiness and success and a sense of community. It means better health if you have been ill. Life will be satisfying, happiness and security is assured. Good relationships or happiness in relationships is foreseen. A secure and harmonious home-life is signified. If you do not dwell on the negative aspects of your life, happiness will ensue. Do not look too far into the future and live and enjoy the present.

Wunjo will surely bring you joy, happiness, harmony, fellowship, prosperity, and peace.

Keywords: Joy, happiness, harmony, success, community, better health, prosperity.

Counsel: Be content with what you have.

Colors: The accompanying colors I have assigned to *Wunjo* are yellow and gold. Yellow and gold are for happiness, joy, and success. Use either for charms and spells.

Hagal's Aett

We do not know anything about the god Hagal. However, some writers and researchers, speculate that he is Heimdall. I believe that Heimdall is a reasonable substitute for Hagal in that he is a guardian, a father of humankind, has insight and vision, and nothing gets past him. He provided strength in adverse situations and appears suited to Hagal's aett. However, he is also linked to the *Mannaz* rune, which is a rune of Tyr.

Heimdall is god of light and the guardian of the gods and of Bifrost the Rainbow Bridge. He is the son of nine mothers. He has amazing vision, and hearing so acute he can hear grass grow and he needs little sleep. At Ragnarok (Armageddon for gods and humans) he and the god Loki are destined to kill each other. He is sometimes called Rig and is said to be the father of all people on earth.

With Hagal's Aett, we will have to work harder to achieve success, but the runes provide the power to do so and we in turn can use our sight, hearing and intuition, to help ourselves. We sometimes also need to apply to a higher power for help in difficult situations. We should watch and listen carefully when runes crop up from this aett, and listen to the inner most symbolic messages that surface to help us.

Hagalaz
Hail — H
Element: Ice

Hail is the whitest of grains.
It whirls from the heavens,
and tossed by gusts of wind, it turns to water.

In this stanza it is clear that the white grain is hail. As it whirls down from the sky and is blown on the wind it melts, as all ice turns to water.

When we have a hail storm it can come without warning and can be short and sharp as it can be painful and damaging. Some hailstorms are soft hail and fall more lightly with small grains of ice. Others are heavy with large grains of ice. Either can happen without warning.

Hagalaz in a reading

You can be assured that whenever *Hagalaz* turns up there will be a crisis. This crisis can be of different proportions. But for sure it means limitations, perhaps caused by something which happened in the past. Your life will feel restricted and possibly thrown into disorder and you perhaps feel you have lost control. Take stock of what is going on in your life. Protect yourself from the storm and be prepared to weather it out. Use the runes to see how you came to be in the situation.

We often have short, sharp, crises in our lives. If *Hagalaz* appears early in a reading, study the runes that follow it to see if the outcome is favorable. Otherwise, throw another cast or pick three more runes to ask for advice to help you through the crisis. This will make you feel better. The crisis can often be short lived, hail soon turns to water. But sometimes you can have crisis after crisis and it seems never to stop. If this happens, it is time to make some life changes to break out of the cycle. But generally with this rune there comes change anyway.

Keywords: Crisis, limitations, restriction, disorder, change.

Counsel: Protect yourself from the storm.

Color: The accompanying color I have assigned to *Hagalaz* is grey. Grey is for uncertainty and confusion. As it is a mixture of black and white it can both absorb and repel.

Nauthiz
Need — N
Element: Fire
Need constricts the chest,
though to children of men it often brings,
help and healing, if heeded in time.

In this stanza we see that along with need comes restriction. This is something that happens to us all. Need constricts our hearts, it strangles the human emotions. The stanza also gives us advice. If we take heed when Nauthiz appears it will help us deal with the problem.

Nauthiz lies between two runes *Hagalaz* and *Isa* with the element of ice, and this gives us the indication that this rune is one of constriction. However, it is an important rune and has a role to play when dealing with crises and difficulties. In a crisis everyone has needs and this is what *Nauthiz* is about; it is the "need" rune. Sometimes we have too many needs. When this is so, we have to face up to and deal with it ourselves. This can take time.

Nauthiz **in a reading**

If *Nauthiz* comes up in a reading, it shows a time of constraints and difficulties. Do not hide from or ignore your problems as it is time to take stock and look at your *real* needs. By facing up to them a solution can be found. Look at what you have to do, prioritize and choose the most important things, and the rest can wait. Do what is necessary to survive. This will also help your stress levels. Sometimes worries add up into a mountain. By putting a little faith in yourself, conserving your energy, and working through it gradually, you will feel better for it. You should try to do this early in those difficult times. There is not an easy way out of this and things will take time to improve. Change is required.

Keywords: Need, constraint, difficulties, help, survival, change.

Counsel: Heed the warning and face up to difficulties. Do not hide from them.

Color: The accompanying color I have assigned to *Nauthiz* is black. Black is for discord, acceptance, change, grounding, and banishing negativity.

|

Isa
Ice — I
Element: Ice
Ice is very cold and vastly slippery.
It glistens like glass, or a jewel,
The ground formed of frost, is a fair to behold.

This stanza tells us of how ice is freezing cold and slippery, and like a gemstone is beautiful to look at. A ground frost is pleasing to the eye.

Here we need to consider what ice is to us. Ice is very cold. In ice we can freeze things solid and it holds fast and has preserved prehistoric animals and ancient man from eons ago. Ice is slippery, but is also beautiful, it glistens like a jewel. We can skate elegantly on ice or slip and fall. Ice cools us down when we get too hot and it sooths a swelling.

Isa in a reading

When *Isa* turns up in a reading do not expect any changes soon. Ice means a freeze out. Everything is frozen, it is static and it has no motion. If you try to walk on it you get nowhere fast.

But ice is beautiful as it is restricting. If your question was about a relationship, you need to look at the reasons you are in that relationship. Is it just because you are proud to be with the person and the relationship is going nowhere, or even just that you are afraid of being alone or a failure? Perhaps there is nothing except shallowness or surface beauty to keep it going. You could be spellbound, so now is the time to look deeper.

This applies to any situation that you are in for the wrong reasons, so think carefully. It is time to look to the future. Think while you wait for the thaw. This is a time to be calm and take stock. Spring is just around the corner. Watch you do not slip around so much you cannot easily get up again. Sometimes it is worthwhile to take the time out to think and plan, and to use ice to your advantage. If you do, you will move forward into a better phase with ease and grace.

Keywords: Ice, stagnation, freeze out, thaw, spellbound, spring.

Counsel: Watch you do not slip and wait for the thaw.

Color: The accompanying color I have assigned to *Isa* is dark-blue. Dark-blue is for inertia, coldness, and suppression.

Jera
Year or Season — J,Y
Element: Earth

The harvest brings hope to man,
If God lets the earth, bestow her bright
fruits on both the rich and the needy.

In this stanza, we see that the harvest is man's hope. God willing, Mother Earth will give up her fruits to everyone, both the rich and the needy. We all need to eat to survive. Our hard work brings in the good harvest.

The harvest brings fruitfulness after hard work. It could be that we have had to exercise patience while we wait for the rewards of our labors. What we now reap can provide income and sustenance. It will keep us provided for in the dark months of winter. Now is the time to give thanks for the bountiful harvest. However, what we sow we can expect to reap.

Jera in a reading
The harvest is a part of the year cycle, and with patience, diligence and also some luck, you will reap what you have sown some months before. You will be blessed with bounty. Prosperity and success are your rewards. You have achieved and are fulfilled.

With this rune you look to what you have worked at and you will see that it was all worth it. The hard work could be success at work or a project you are working on, it could be a relationship you have worked at. Perhaps you have studied hard or are just awaiting results after a patient wait for something. Whatever, it is a time of waiting which will be soon be over. Of course it depends on where *Jera* shows up in the reading as to how long you will have to wait for those results.

If *Jera* appears in a cast among runes of crisis, be careful you are not now reaping what you have sown some time before. Think carefully about what could have led you into your present situation.

If things have been going wrong for you or you are in need, you can expect some help at last with *Jera*.

Keywords: Harvest, bounty, prosperity, success, achievement, patience.

Counsel: Remember that you reap what you sow.

Colors: The accompanying colors I have assigned to *Jera* are green and brown. Green is for harvest, wealth, abundance and growth. Brown is for practical matters, harvest and endurance. For magical purposes green is the more important.

Eihwaz
Yew — E, I, EI
Element: All elements
The yew is outwardly a rough tree.
Held hard and fast in the earth, it is the guardian of fire.
Deeply the roots twist. It is a joy on the estate.

In this stanza we read about the yew. On the outside it is rough and held fast in the earth, and it guards the fire. Its roots twist deep beneath it and it is a joy to look upon.

Yew is the tree of immortality as it symbolizes death and rebirth. It has the power of renewal. New grows out of the old. This was sometimes called the tree of death as it is grown in graveyards. But as the possible World Tree it is a route to heaven. The fire within is holy, purifying and renewing. It is a rebirth on a higher level and is protective.

Eihwaz in a reading

Where there is death there is also new life. Old things must die for new ones to begin, as it is part of the cycle of life. Look at what in your past is affecting the here and now and try to resolve it. You are in a period of transition, not quite finished with one phase but soon to begin another. Clean out what is old and unnecessary ready for the new phase.

The transition could be a spiritual or personal one. You are about to cross over from the darkness into the welcoming light.

If things are not going so well it could be that they will improve soon. Prepare for this, renewal is just around the corner.

Eihwaz offers protection, reliability, and a steadfast quiet strength. It is a defensive rune and will also protect.

Keywords: Immortality, renewal, rebirth, protection, transition, reliability, steadfastness, quiet strength.

Counsel: Old things must die for the new ones to begin, so prepare.

Colors: The accompanying colors I have assigned to *Eihwaz* are green and white. Green is for growth and fertility. White is for purity, protection and truth. Use both colors for charms and spells.

Perthro
Gambling or Gaming Cup — P
Element: Water
Gaming is always play and laughter,
among bold men and where warriors sit,
in the beer hall in merriment together.

In this stanza gaming is play and laughter among the brave warriors in the hall, a place of community, comradeship, and solidarity.

For us this indicates a time of enjoyment and pleasure with friends. We all need to socialize and just relax and enjoy life. To do this we should leave worries and insecurity behind and not withdraw from companionship. Life can get stuck in a rut and sometimes it is necessary to take a risk. Perthro is viewed as a female rune and linked with the *Norns* the mistresses of fate.

Perthro in a reading

Perthro the gambling rune is not an unwelcome sight, and it has been linked with the Norns, the goddesses of fate. But at times it is difficult to comprehend.

Now is the time to take a gamble on life. It is game of fortune or chance but the risk is a calculated one. Obstacles will be overcome. A hopeless position becomes a promising one. Luck in battle or actions can be expected.

It is a creative and inspiring rune, so a good time for creative ideas is indicated. You may have to make a decision you are not totally sure about. But the fates are with you. *Perthro* is a lucky rune and also often viewed as a female rune; if you are male it could mean that someone is coming into your life. Regardless, it is a time to be bold and to maybe take the plunge.

Whatever comes to you it will involve joy, pleasure, and laughter. Relax and enjoy what is offered. Good company along the road is the shortest cut.

Keywords: Gamble, community, comradeship, solidarity, enjoyment, pleasure, risk, chance, creativity, luck, boldness.

Counsel: Be bold and take the plunge.

Colors: The accompanying colors I have assigned to *Perthro* are silver and white. Silver is the color of the moon, female intuition and energy. White is creativity, attracting positive energy and divine inspiration. Use both colors for charms and spells.

Algiz
Elk — Z

Element: Air

The elk sedge grows most often in the marsh,
It waxes in water, and grimly wounds
And makes red with blood, any man who dares to grasp it.

The elk sedge grass, like the antlers of the elk, is both sharp and dangerous. The elk sedge grass grows in water and wounds by cutting you if you dare to grab it.

Algiz is perhaps the most difficult rune to understand. Sedge grass can rip our fingers if we try to grab it. The sharp blades of grass are representative of a two-edged sword, so there is a warning here to be on our guard. Fools rush in where angels fear to tread.

Algiz also represents through the elk's antlers, spiritual growth, or spiritual rebirth. It is solitary, so this is a passage we will have to face alone and something we will need to carefully consider. Divine forces are at work.

Algiz in a reading

Watch out for unseen influences in your life, there is danger around you, be wary and cautious and follow your instincts and you will win through. *Algiz* is there to protect you and wisdom is provided. Look out for someone coming into your life that is a good influence, a mentor, teacher or wise counsel.

A struggle between light and darkness is indicated, but you are protected. The symbol of *Algiz* resembles a guardian angel and does have powerful protective powers. The elk's antlers will ward off evil. Wear or carry the symbol as a talisman.

Keywords: Caution, protection, advice, wisdom, talisman.

Counsel: Danger is around you. Be wary and follow your instincts to win through.

Colors: The accompanying colors I have assigned to *Algiz* are white and purple. White is truth, purity, and protection. Purple is spiritual energy, wisdom, and psychic awareness. For magical purposes use both colors.

Sowilo
Sun — S
Element: Air

The sun is by seamen, always hoped for,
When they sail over the fishes' bath,
Until the sea horse, they bring to land.

In this stanza we read that the sun is always hoped for by sailors as they sail across the oceans, until the ship is brought safely to land.

The sun is warming, life-giving, provides light. It is light in the darkness and rises every morning. When we wake up to sunshine after a period of dull weather, it lifts our hearts. We often feel optimistic and capable of doing anything. We know where we are when we see the sun, as at midday it is in the south, so it is directional. All the planets of our solar system revolve around the sun. The earth herself is dependent on the sun for life as we are.

Sowilo in a reading

Sowilo the sun is a very positive force in your life or about to come into your life. You have the power to make changes. You life is illuminated and the sun is upon you lighting your way to success and happiness. *Sowilo* is belief, optimism, and confidence in yourself. It is an easy journey, perhaps of personal growth. Higher cosmic forces are entering your life and in this you are blessed. Be careful not to block the sun out of your life, accept it and let it guide you.

In rising every morning and setting every evening, the sun is a constant rebirth, so this is a good time for new beginnings and new projects.

The sun is encouraging as it is nourishing and warming, and is the summer banishing the winter and melting any ice. It is a beacon of hope and a guide to a safe harbor.

Keywords: Sun, light, optimism, direction, life-force, success, happiness, confidence, rebirth, new beginnings, encouraging, warming, nourishing, banishing, guide.

Counsel: Be careful not to block the sun out of your life, accept it and let it guide you.

Colors: The accompanying colors I have assigned to *Sowilo* are yellow and gold. Both yellow and gold are symbolic of the sun. Yellow is for happiness, optimism, luck, confidence and creativity. Gold is for higher spirituality, inner strength, happiness and creativity. Use either or both for magical purposes.

Tyr's Aett

Tyr is the hero god of War, glory, victory, and courage. His Roman counterpart is Mars and his day is Tuesday. He is a warrior god, and of victory in battle. He is one-handed as he put his hand in to mouth of the wolf Fenrir as a gesture of good will, indicating his courage and sacrifice. He is the god of law and justice.

Tyr's Aett is a solid one. It has runes of doing, achieving, and for establishing order in your life. Tyr's Aett helps build solid foundations. Runes from this group are essential in the running of our everyday lives. We have to work for our security, and we have to endure the ups and downs that life brings

Tiwaz
Warrior — T
Element: Air
Tir is a sign that holds loyalty well,
with the nobles; on its straight course,
over night's mists, it is unfailing.

This stanza tells us that Tir (Tiwaz) is a sign of the holding of oaths of fidelity by the nobles, it holds true on its course even in the mists of night.

Tiwaz as the arrow or spear is pointing the way straight and true, as a star never fails to holds its course in the night sky. It is the rune of the warrior god Tyr and he was once the chief Norse deity and came before Odin, but was eventually relegated. His good qualities endured, and he remains to champion and guide us in battle.

Tiwaz in a reading
You will not get lost with *Tiwaz* in your reading. It indicates courage, confidence and trust, and success in legal matters, which also indicates that you have, or are soon to have, a battle on your hands.

If it is justice you are looking for, then you should get it in some way with this rune. It points the way to victory in disputes. *Tiwaz* will help you summon up the strength to fight in your own or perhaps in someone else's battle. You are protected. It can also mean that good advice perhaps from someone of the legal profession is about to be offered.

Stand your ground and do not compromise your principles. Do not break sworn oaths, but honor promises and act justly, reliably and wisely. As with Tyr who sacrificed his hand, self-sacrifice might be necessary. *Tiwaz* will guide you in this.

In relationships *Tiwaz* also points the way. It indicates good and strong relations between couples, or a romance on the way.

Tiwaz is a rune of truth, strength, courage, and light in the darkness.

Keywords: Warrior, guide, justice, victory, strength, protection, wise counsel, reliability, honor, wisdom, self-sacrifice, courage, light in the darkness.

Counsel: Stand your ground and do not compromise your principles.

Colors: The accompanying colors I have assigned to *Tiwaz* are red, orange, and blue. Red is for vitality, energy, courage, survival and power. Orange is for strength success, confidence, achieving goals and legal matters. Blue is for honesty, wisdom, and communication. Use red or orange with blue, or all three colors, for charms and spells.

Berkano
Birch — B
Element: Earth
The birch is fruitless, still it bears
twigs without fertile seed, its shining branches
high on its crown loaded with leaves, reach to the sky.

In this stanza we read that the birch has no shoots and bears no fertile fruit. Its beautiful shining branches with their abundance of leaves, reach to the sky.

The birch tree is a tree which signifies awakening and the return of spring and fertility to the land. It is associated with the maiden aspect of the goddess and with the waxing and fertile moon. The besom was made of birch and in past times, couples jumped over it to legally be declared married. These days it is still used in spiritual weddings called handfastings. The birch is a tree of Ogham, and is the tree for the first month of the year which begins at the Celtic festival Samhain, now commonly known as Hallowe'en. The besom was also used for purifying and to sweep out the old year.

Berkano in a reading

Berkano is the rune of birth, new beginnings and new starts. With this rune you can reach for the sky. It is the rune of baby projects and projects in their infancy, in other words there are new beginnings for whatever subjects you are asking about. These are often endeavors that grow out of nothing. Look after your "new baby" as with anything new it will require nurturing so it can thrive.

A time of fertility is ahead. Couples jump the besom of birch to reinforce their marriage vows and also for luck, as the birch is a symbol of new relationships. If you are in a new relationship, things will go well. This also applies to success in careers. If you do not have this yet it will come.

Birch twigs have long been used as a tool of cleansing and purifying. Sweep out the old to welcome in the new.

Keywords: Birch, spring, fertility, purification, new beginnings, luck, success.

Counsel: Sweep out the old to welcome in the new.

Colors: The accompanying colors I have assigned to *Berkano* are green and yellow. Green is for fertility, growth, abundance and good luck. Yellow is symbolic of newness (daffodils and primroses in spring, and chicks). For magical purposes use both colors.

Ehwaz
Horse — E
Element: Earth
The horse before earls, a noble's pleasure.
Proud on its hooves, around it wealthy heroes
exchange speech. Ever a comfort to the restless.

In this stanza, we learn that owning a horse is a pleasure for the nobles. When the heroes are on their horses talking to each other, the horse's hooves are bold. The horse is a comfort to the restless.

Ehwaz is a rune of partnerships, progress, movement and general mobility. Man and his horse have always been a good partnership. In the past, the horse was essential to carry man to his destinations as quickly as possible, yet he was also a good companion to him. The horse and the man have a strong bond. The horse has spirit so keep in under your control.

Ehwaz in a reading

With *Ehwaz* you can expect a journey. This can be a literal one or a metaphorical one. And for the restless, those who are eager to get on, you can expect rapid progress in your affairs.

The horse is a vehicle and you will have the means for traveling or for moving forward in your life. You will also have the courage and energy to see projects through.

A good, strong, and harmonious partnership is indicted, this can be a life partner, a good friendship, or a career or work partner. But you can expect help and to give the same help in return to benefit you both.

Get to know your *fylgja* or *fetch* so that you it can help you communicate between the worlds (see more in Chapter 5) and assist you on your life journey.

Keywords: Partnerships, progress, movement, mobility, bonding, journey, vehicle, success.

Counsel: The horse has spirit so keep in under your control.

Colors: The accompanying colors I have assigned to *Ehwaz* are blue and pink. Blue is for harmony, peace, loyalty, honesty, and communication. Pink is for friendships and also binds. Use whichever suits you purposes best. Orange or red can be used as an addition for strength and courage depending on the purpose.

Mannaz

Man — M

Element: Air

Man in his joy, is dear to his kinsmen,
Though each shall have to part from the other,
when by the Lord's judgment he is entrusted to the earth.

In this stanza we read that man in his laughter is dear to his relatives and friends. But one day they will be parted by death and committed to the earth.

Mannaz is the rune of humankind and is linked to the god Heimdall. It is the person or the Self. Man is not infallible, we are born, we live, and then we die in the cycle of life and death that none of us can avoid. Yet we are all in the same boat, and with that is a sense of comradeship, community, shared experience and mutual compassion.

Mannaz in a reading

Mannaz is a rune of consciousness and logic. If you want to progress, you often have to gather the help or support from among your friends and relatives, as you help them in return. You also need to look at your own position in the community, show compassion and do not neglect friends and loved ones. Try to work or interact with people too in times of trouble or to achieve your objective. It is also important to use your own natural talents and skills to their best advantage.

The time is right for personal inner progress in the way of discovery of the Self; you can do this by facing your weaknesses and recognizing your innate talents.

Keywords: Man, Self, comradeship, community, compassion, talents, skills, inner progress.

Counsel: Do not neglect loved ones. Use your own natural talents and skills.

Colors: The accompanying colors I have assigned to *Mannaz* are green and brown. Green and brown are both earthly colors and are grounding. Green is for growth, love, fertility, and abundance. Brown is for practical matters and sense of home. Use either or both for charms or spells.

Laguz
Lake — L
Water is to folk thought endless when they sail forth
on an unstable ship. The great waves of the sea terrify,
And the seahorse heeds not the bridle.
Element: Water

In this stanza we learn how treacherous the sea can be. An ocean journey is long, especially on an unsteady ship. The strong waves of the sea can be terrifying and the ship is not always under control.

Laguz is the lake, water and the ocean. The waves of the ocean or the sea are sometimes soft and gentle, but in a storm they toss the boat around. This is the water of life. Water will always go the quickest way, if this is over a cliff in the form of a waterfall, than this is so. White-water rivers can be found flowing fast and turbulent. Healing waters flow underground in secret springs and Holy wells, which can benefit us. Water is used to bless babies at birth.

Laguz in a reading

Water represents the emotions, and with *Laguz* moods can be wavering. In life we have ups and downs, everyone does, but sometimes things can seem overwhelming. Watch you do not go under the waves or over the waterfall. Be flexible and float and do not be rigid as you are likely to sink. You have the energies to adapt and go with the flow. Ride the waves and you will overcome any problems and will not get seasick. With *Laguz* you have the ability to do this. Use the water to your benefit; it can be therapeutic. It can also help you move forward although this could be a long journey.

With *Laguz* there will be forward movement but with perhaps minor delays and a few rough moments.

Keywords: Emotions, flexibility, journey, energies, forward movement.

Counsel: Watch you do not go under the waves, go with the flow.

Colors: The accompanying colors I have assigned to *Laguz* are blue, green, and silver. Blue is symbolic of water. It is the color of the sea and is calming. Green is also a sea color and is representative of the emotions of the heart. Silver is of the moon and tides. It is protection and intuition. For magical purposes use a combination of colors that suit the purpose of charm or spell.

Ingwaz
God Ing — NG
Element: Water/Earth
Ing was first seen among the East Danes, until
eastward he went over the waves, with his wagon,
And thus the warriors named the hero.

This stanza tells us about a god called Ing. He was first seen by the East Danes. One day he went back eastwards with his wagon over the sea, and the warriors themselves named the hero.

Ing was an ancient fertility god. Some say he is either identified with, or actually is, Frey. He drove around in his wagon blessing the land in the springtime. In the spring nothing has started to grow yet. We plant the seeds, encourage their growth and wait for them to flourish. Later we can harvest.

Ingwaz in a reading
Ingwaz can mean the germ of a project that you need to nurture along or patiently have to wait around for, to get or see the results. A new phase or start is indicated. It is a quiet time for now, but later you will reap the rewards if you prepare. Clear the decks, tidy the ground ready for planting. Take time out to think or to review the situation, then you can start.

You are being shown the right way to do this and strength and energy will gradually build to see it through.

Ingwaz is also a strong male rune, and there may come a strong male influence in your life or a romance at the very beginning of what is to be a longer relationship.

Keywords: Fertile time, spring, seed, new growth, new phase or start, new relationship or romance.

Counsel: Clear the decks, tidy the ground ready for planting.

Color: The accompanying color I have assigned to *Ingwaz* is green. Green is for fertility, growth, abundance, and future harvest.

Dagaz
Day/Daybreak — D
Element: Fire/Air
Day is the Lord's messenger, dear to man,
The leaders great light, a joy and hope
to rich and poor, is a benefit to all.

Day is the messenger of the Lord, and holds dear to man. The great light brings hope and merriment, and is for everyone to enjoy, both rich and poor.

Dagaz is the dawn of a brand new day and can be identified with the season of spring. It can indicate a new start or change for the better. It is also the dawning of day, daybreak when the first rays of the sun shine upon the earth, bringing light. In bringing the light, Day chases away Night or darkness.

In Norse mythology, the All-Father Odin put Dagur to light up the sky. Dagur is bright and beautiful taking after his paternal ancestry and his chariot is pulled by the horse Skinfaxi. His father is Delling (Twilight) and his mother is Nott (Night) who black and swarthy drives across the night sky, her chariot pulled by the horse Hrimfaxi.

Dagaz in a reading
With *Dagaz* you can see clearly what is required so you can move onward with a feeling of optimism. As day chases away the dark

night, daylight will prevail. This is a period of transition and a turning point for you. You can start again with hope of success if this is needed.

Revelations of things that were previously hidden to you andwhich could help you understand a problem, could be indicated. In times of great stress you retain hope, and the new day brings an uplifting feeling, anything is possible.

You can be assured that night will fall again at some point, but not before you have had the time to enjoy the moment and plan for the future.

In spiritual matters, *Dagaz* can mean an awakening or enlightenment.

Keywords: Hope, merriment, new start, change, transition, light, optimism, success, revelation, enlightenment.

Counsel: Enjoy the moment and plan for the future.

Color: The accompanying color I have assigned to *Dagaz* is yellow. Yellow is for spring, success, happiness, optimism and the sun (light).

Othala
Homestead — O
The estate is dear to every man.
If he can take pleasure in what he has,
More often will prosper.
Element: Earth

The homestead is very dear to every man. If he safeguards what is precious in his life, he will prosper.

Othala is to do with the home situation, your estate, inheritance, your possessions and your family. It is your country or place you feel is home, your town, village, community or extended family. It is both the inner you and the outer you.

Othala in a reading

When *Othala* appears in a cast it means that things are established and you have or will have peace and prosperity. You have security around you. Friends will help you if needed.

Perhaps a new home is indicated or a move or even that you will inherit something. But whatever it is you can be assured of the security you will receive from it. Learn to appreciate and enjoy what you have. If you keep things harmonious in the home and community then prosperity will surely come. Keep grounded. Safeguard your inheritances. Remember that home is where the heart is.

In spiritual matters, your body is the refuge of the spirit. Look after the casing and do not neglect your health. Treasure yourself and take care of the inner you.

Keywords: Estate, inheritance, possessions, family, country, community, peace, prosperity, security, harmony, grounding, safeguarding.

Counsel: Learn to appreciate and enjoy what you have. Treasure yourself.

Colors: The accompanying colors I have assigned to *Othala* are brown and green. Brown and green are earthly colors. Brown is for practical matters, endurance, harvest, and home. Green is for possessions, wealth, love, healing, growth and fertility. Use either or both for charms and spells.

Table 4.1
Runes and Keywords

ᚠ   Fehu   Wealth, possessions, good fortune, prosperity, sharing, luck, fertility

ᚢ   Uruz   Strength, stamina, energy, fortitude, tenacity, independence, passion, luck, creativity, courage, good health, happiness

ᚦ   Thurisaz   Protective, forces of nature, tribulation, adversity, survival of difficulties, self-assertion.

ᚨ   Ansuz   Communication, wisdom, life-breath, inner voice, teaching, inspiration, persuasion, contentment

ᚱ   Raidho   Journey, excitement, pleasure, adventure, transportation, change, movement, new experiences

ᚲ   Kenaz   Creative ventures, illumination, heightened sexual passion

ᚷ   Gebo   Gift, happiness, praise, support, honor, nourishment.

ᚹ   Wunjo   Joy, happiness, harmony, success, community, better health, prosperity

ᚺ   Hagalaz   Crisis, limitations, restriction, disorder, change

ᚾ	Nauthiz	Need, constraint, difficulties, help, survival, change
ᛁ	Isa	Ice, stagnation, freeze out, thaw, spellbound, spring
ᛃ	Jera	Harvest, bounty, prosperity, success, achievement, patience
ᛇ	Eihwaz	Immortality, renewal, rebirth, protection, transition, reliability, steadfastness, quiet strength
ᛈ	Perthro	Gamble, community, comradeship, solidarity, enjoyment, pleasure, risk, chance, creativity, luck, boldness
ᛉ	Algiz	Caution, protection, advice, wisdom, talisman.
ᛋ	Sowilo	Sun, light, optimism, direction, life-force, success, happiness, confidence, rebirth, new beginnings, encouraging, warming, nourishing, banishing, guide.
ᛏ	Tiwaz	Warrior, guide, justice, victory, strength, protection, wise counsel, reliability, honor, wisdom, self-sacrifice, courage, light in the darkness.
ᛒ	Berkano	Birch, spring, fertility, purification, new beginnings, luck, success.

ᛗ Ehwaz   Partnerships, progress, movement, mobility, bonding, journey, vehicle, success.

ᛗ Mannaz   Man, Self, comradeship, community, compassion, talents, skills, inner progress.

ᛚ Laguz   Emotions, flexibility, journey, energies, forward movement.

◇ Ingwaz   Fertile time, spring, seed, new growth, new phase or start, new relationship or romance.

ᛞ Dagaz   Hope, merriment, new start, change, transition, light, optimism, success, revelation, enlightenment.

ᛟ Othala   Estate, inheritance, possessions, family, country, community, peace, prosperity, security, harmony, grounding, safeguarding.

Chapter 5

Psychology and Cosmology

Psychology of the Runes

When we cast the runes, they open unseen pathways between our conscious and unconscious self (our psyche) in predicting what lies ahead. Our own instincts and knowledge from the unconscious helps us in reading and understanding the runes often without us realizing. As we read the rune symbols, thoughts pop into our minds even though we might not be aware from where these thoughts come, but our instincts tell us they are correct. Subsequently, these intuitive skills will become stronger and more successful over time. The runes develop them by continually tapping into wisdom lying deep in the unconscious mind, revealing hidden truths and acting as a messenger bring them forth into the conscious mind. Carl Gustav Jung the psychologist called this wisdom, "archetypes of the collective unconscious".

Jungian Terms

When reading books on the runes you will often encounter the terms mentioned above such as "archetypes", "the collective unconscious", "Individuation" and the "Self" among others. All these terms come from Carl Jung. Quite often the terms are used to signify the meaning of certain runes, such as Mannaz which connects to the "Self" and also to "Individuation". So it is handy to familiarize ourselves with them. When studying any divination it is useful to read Jung. There are many easy to understand books which outline his basic theories, and I recommend his book Man and his Symbols, which was written by his friends (fellow psychologists), and edited by himself. It was written to be accessible by the "man in the street" rather than purely for academics. Below I talk about two Jungian concepts. You will find the Glossary of the Psyche as termed by Jung at the end of the book.

Synchronicity

I write here about synchronicity as it is quite significant when it comes to understanding the hidden mysteries of the runes. A synchronous event is one which is more than an ordinary coincidence and cannot be explained. It is when two or more outside events coincide with a psychic event. Some of these events at times include archetypal symbols, are often numinous, and sometimes there are accompanying dreams. These events happened separately and neither causes the other.

When we read the runes, we look at the symbols (the outside event) and they reveal to us the underlying but hidden psychic forces. Another way of explaining this is to say in the microcosm or rune symbols, we open our minds to the macrocosm or omnipresent energies, we would not normally recognize. These universal energies reveal past, present, and future events. The future events are not necessarily fixed, and by reading the runes and revealing the possibilities we can change patterns, or at least adapt ourselves to them. So, in essence we are acknowledging that mind and matter are harmonizing aspects of the same reality.

So how do we recognize a synchronous event? The best way to help you understand theses events is by giving examples.

When I was young I was in church on Good Friday with my father and sister. It was a church close to where my father lived and therefore we only went there when visiting him. The church had a beautiful altar, with pictures of the saints above it and they were all covered in purple boards. I looked at the boards and remembered that the end one, on the second row at the left side, fell off when I had been in church with my father and sister also on a Good Friday a few years before. As I was looking at the board and recalling my memory, it promptly fell off, scaring the life out of me. So why did it happen at exactly the moment I was recalling the memory from several years before? Evidently because there were other forces at work here relating mind with matter.

Another event that could be called synchronistic is when my mother was once not feeling very well when visiting the grave of my stepfather's parents. My stepfather was tidying the grave, and my mother was watching. She looked around her and behind was a beautiful grave that was sadly neglected. A lone woman occupied the grave. Even though my mother was feeling unwell, she thought it was a terrible shame and decided to tidy it. She noted the woman's name. Later as my parents walked on through the cemetery, my mother having worn herself out needed to sit down to rest. They came across a bench with a name on it. Sitting down my mother looked behind her and was startled to see it was dedicated to the same woman who was in the grave she had just tidied. Here a psychic event coincided or connected with a normal event to enable the occupant of the grave to repay my mother's thoughtfulness in the form of a rest.

These synchronous events are such that we never forget them as they are so significant. People we tell them to also remember them and pass the story on, simply because they are meaningful. Not so long ago at a wedding, my sister-in-law reminded me of the above event. She had also retained the memory of my mother's experience, even though it happened years before. We remember events like this it because it shows us that there are forces at work that we might not fully understand. Still, we acknowledge they exist.

So to sum up, if we learn to recognize and acknowledge these moments, we can explore them instead of writing them off as perhaps just a big coincidence. We then come to accept that there are things that cannot be scientifically explained, as it is impossible that they could have occurred purely by chance. The universe is not just made up of scientific facts. We do not know everything purely because we live in an enlightened age, and we can only benefit from opening our minds to the infinite possibilities. If we delve deeper into the interrelation between mind and matter, or spirit and matter, it will in turn help us in developing our relationship with the runes.

The Self

All the components of the psyche, (listed in the glossary at the end of this book) make up the whole Self. Getting to know that whole or "Self" is what Carl Jung calls *Individuation*.

The runes can help you get in touch with those parts of the Self that we do not know well. And we have to face and understand that we have parts of us that we do not necessarily like, but by facing up to them, we go a long way to finding our way to the Self.

When we cast the runes, we look into the Self. We learn that the world cannot be perfect, but with the advice of the wise runes we can take control of our destiny and face the dark and destructive side of life and get through it, as there is always a brighter and better side of life to look forward to.

Just as we have many different aspects and parts that make up the whole or the "Self", each and every root and the trunk and branches, is an essential part of the tree of life called "Yggdrasil". And just likes the parts of the Self make up our own cosmology or inner universe, the nine worlds of Yggdrasil make up the Norse cosmology.

Yggdrasil the World Tree

In Norse Mythology, Yggdrasil is the world tree and is usually accepted to be a gigantic ash, but some recent research suggests it was possibly a yew tree as the World Tree was said to be evergreen. Yggdrasil connects all the nine worlds of Norse cosmology.

Yggdrasil acts as a metaphor for our own being. The cosmology of the tree works together as one whole. All the different worlds are part of that whole. When we study the runes we tap into the part of ourselves not often reached, the unconscious or psyche. We therefore begin to understand more about our own cosmology, in other words about the different parts of us that makes up our being.

The Nine Worlds of Yggdrasil

You will find the names of these worlds differ from source to source, so I use the ones most commonly mentioned with modern spellings. The worlds are on three different levels and it is not certain exactly how they are placed, so it is up to the individual to work out something that they believe is logical. This is my own version.

Asgard, Alfheim and *Vanaheim* rest on the branches of Yggdrasil in the upper world. Asgard is the home of the warlike gods the Aesir, ruled by Odin. Alfheim is the home of the light elves and ruled by Frey. Vanaheim is the home of the Vanir gods who are connected with nature and fertility.

Below and connected to the upper world by Bifrost the Rainbow Bridge is *Midgard* which is the home of humanity, the land of men. It is surrounded by an ocean, which is the home of Jormungand the serpent. *Jotunheim* is the home of the Jotuns or frost giants and their stronghold which is called Utgard. It lays to the west of Midgard. Somewhere below lays *Svartalfheim*, the world of the dark elves or dwarfs.

Muspelheim lies in the lower realms and is the home of the fire giants. *Niflheim* is a frozen wasteland, a land of ice and fog, and is ruled by the goddess Hel. The final realm is *Hel* or *Helheim* which is the land of the dead. Hel is not to be confused with the Christian Hell. It is the land of the ordinary dead (of those not killed nobly in battle). It is the land of the ancestors.

Three roots support the trunk of Yggdrasil. There is continuing discussion as to where these wells and indeed the roots lie. This is owing to the information being taken from a vast variety of sources of mythology and diverse interpretations of it.

The following explanations are taken from Snorri Sturluson's *The Prose Edda*. However, other sources place all the wells in the lower realms, presumably Hel, Niflheim, and Muspelheim.

The sacred *Well of Urd* is said to lie beneath the root that passes through the heavens, presumably Asgard, and beneath it dwell the Norns.

Beneath the root that passes through Jotunheim is said to lay the *Well of Mimir*, (also called the Well of Knowledge). The well is named after the wise god Mimir who guards and drinks from it gaining insight. Although the myth is fragmentary, it is said that Odin sacrificed one of his eyes in exchange for drinking from the well to gain inspiration, wisdom, and the power of vision.

Beneath the root that passes through Niflheim, the *Well of Hvergelmir* is said to lie. It is called the roaring cauldron and is the mother-fountain of all waters.

There are many creatures that reside in the tree. On the top sits an eagle (sometimes called a rooster), and sitting upon its forehead is a hawk called Vedrfolnir. The roots of Niflheim were gnawed at by a dragon called Nidhogg, and a squirrel called Ratatosk runs up and down the tree. And four stags or harts feed on the bark of Yggdrasil and they are called Duneyr, Durathror, Dvalin, and Dain.

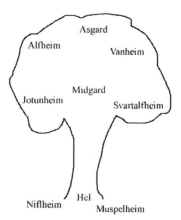

Yggdrasil

The runes work on three levels, the spiritual, earthly (of humanity), and unconscious (or underworld).

The spiritual level can be reached by meditation, visualization, shamanistic journeys, invoking or evoking gods, religion, psychic communication, and of course we have the Spirit residing within us. The realms of the spiritual level are Asgard, Alfheim and Vanaheim, the realms of the Aesir gods of heaven, the light elves, and the Vanir gods of nature.

The earthly level is the easiest to reach as we are already there. Things are more open and clear to us. It is the realm of humanity and of the earthly, practical, and materials things of our world, which we deal with every day. The realms of the earthly level are Midgard, Jotunheim and Svartalfheim, the realms of humankind, frost giants, and dark elves.

The unconscious level is reached by getting in touch with the anima/animus and the shadow parts of the Self (see Jungian glossary), facing up to and confronting our weaknesses, and recognizing archetypes and symbols. The runes will also help us reach deep into this level. The realms of the unconscious level are Muspelheim, Niflheim and Hel, the lands of fire, ice and fog, and the underworld.

Human Cosmology

To correspond with Yggdrasil there is the human cosmology. Yggdrasil has the magical number of nine worlds to make up the whole of its cosmology, and so too does the human cosmology have nine aspects. As with positioning, the matching to the realms of Yggdrasil is open to speculation, and below is my version.

Ondh or *Ond* is the life breath of the cosmos in which we share. *Hamingja* is our protection, our guardian, and is also luck and fortune. We can inherit it and in turn it can be inherited by our descendants. The *Fylgja* is an etheric self which is connected to us but operates separately, and which for instance can travel on the astral plane. It is otherwise known as the *Fetch* and is likely to take the form of an animal to do this. It may represent the character of the person it is attached to. Odin for instance, was always accompanied by two wolves; perhaps these were representative of his courageous nature. If we can get in touch with our fylgja or fetch, we can call on it to aid us in our general lives and with magic. The fylgja both communicates with and carries messages between worlds. It stays with us all our lives and dies with us.

You can use Visualization Exercise 3 at the end of this chapter to help you discover what form your fetch is likely to take.

Lik or *Likr* is the physical shell of the human body. *Hugr* or *Hughr* is the part of the mind which gives the power of thought and perception (the conscious). And *Minni* is the part of the conscious which retains memory.

Sal or *Saflr* is the ghost or after death image. *Hamr* is the part of the mind that gives image to the body or *Lik*. Lastly, *Odhr* is the sense of inspiration.

The aspects of our spirituality or higher consciousness are Ondh, Hamingja and Fylgja. The aspects of the earthly level or consciousness are Lik, Hugr and Minni. And the aspects of the unconscious are Sal, Hamr and Odhr.

Among the runes we will find spiritual ones such as *Algiz* and *Eihwaz*; practical ones relating to earthly matter such as *Mannaz*, *Jera*, and *Othala*, and those relating to the unconscious such as *Kenaz*, *Isa*, *Hagalaz*, and *Nauthiz*.

We can reach all the levels by our use of the runes. As we get to know the runes better, we come to an understanding with them and become familiar with the different levels on which they act.

Ond

Hamingja   Fylgja

Lik

Hugr   Minni

Sal

Hamr   Odhr

Human Cosmology

Visualization Exercise 2

Here is a second visualization exercise, to help you further that connection with your runes. Please follow the preparation described in Visualization 1.

You are walking along the forest path. There is a mystical feel to the forest today. You can see the early morning mist floating in swirls among the autumn tinted trees and bushes. The leaves lay in a crisp golden carpet beneath your feet and there is a fresh nip to the air. The autumn sun filters through the trees revealing a kaleidoscope of vibrant red, burnished gold, flaming orange and jade. A fresh breeze sways the boughs, sending large leaves floating through the air like golden snow. As you walk, your feet stir up a lovely earthy, woodsy smell from beneath your feet.

The path winds ahead, and in the distance you can hear trickling water, and you know that soon you will find the stream and the waterfall. You continue along the path and a squirrel collecting the fruits of the autumn scurries up a tree. You stroll on taking note of everything you see, hear, and smell.

The path is widening in front of you and soon you meet the running water and you walk onwards knowing the waterfall is just ahead. You look for the big flat stone on which to sit and wait.

You sit on your stone and after a while you see a movement to the side of you. Someone is coming along the path in the opposite direction. It is a tall old man dressed in a blue cloak and a wide-brimmed hat. He has grey hair and a long grey beard. You wait for him. This is the wise man.

He smiles at you but does not speak. You stand up and face him. He opens his hand and in it lays a rune. He holds it out to you. You reach out and take it.

Does he speak to you? What does he say? Do you pick up his thoughts?

He smiles and walks away.

You sit back on your stone. Now you are very aware of the rune in your hand. Did you see a symbol on it? Whether you did or not, how does the rune make you feel? What are your immediate feelings? Are they positive or negative feelings? Is this a protective rune perhaps, or a rune of good fortune?

Think about it for a while.

Take two or three deep breaths and slowly open your eyes. Give yourself a few moments to recover. Take your rune bag and with your power hand choose a rune from it. Does the rune you have chosen mirror the rune that the wise man gave you? Regardless of whether it does or does not, reflect on your chosen rune for a while. Is there a connection between your feelings, any present worries or hopes, what you felt or saw by the waterfall and the rune in your hand? Let these thought and feelings advise you. Now look up the rune meaning if necessary. The rune you have chosen will be your guide for the day.

Visualization Exercise 3

This exercise is to help you connect with you fylgja or fetch and to aid you in your general life, with magic and with divination.

A long time ago, I decided to try to get in touch with my fetch. I used the forest exercise to do this, as it was my favorite visualization. As it happened it worked very well, mainly because I went into a natural trance state. This was easier for me as I have been able to astral project since I was a child (at first this was a natural occurrence and later I taught myself how to do this at will). However, you should only use a trance state if you are experienced. Nevertheless, the exercise should still be successful, especially if you have been practicing the previous two. It is a straightforward exercise.

For me, this is how it worked. I was deep in the forest; suddenly I could see myself separately. I looked completely different than I actually do. I was much younger, and had long fair hair plaited in two pigtails hanging in front of my shoulders. I was wearing peasant dress or at least clothes from long ago. I had my arm stretched up and over a great white ox. Then I became that girl. I could feel the warmth of the ox, its back standing as high as my shoulder. It had great curved horns, and I could see that its short coat was in wonderful condition and shone.

This is why for me *Uruz* has a connection. Strength is something we all need from time to time. I was not surprised to see an ox, and instinctively I had already suspected this was my fetch.

Perhaps you too know instinctively which animal or creature is your fetch. You can also use Visualization 3 to connect with your power animal. Your power animal is there to help you in daily matters depending on the animal, and you might have more than one. It is possible that the same one keeps recurring perhaps this is your fetch, or you lack the quality it provides. Each animal offers you different qualities you have need of at that present time, such as strength, memory, shrewdness, wisdom and optimism.

While you can use your fylgja or fetch for communicating between worlds and for magical purposes, you can use your power animal along with an appropriate rune to give you assistance as you face troubles.

Please follow the preparations in Visualization 1.

Imagine yourself entering the forest. The forest lies close to the sea. If you instinctively feel it is the rainforest you should be in, then that should be so and the squirrel, deer, bear or wolf, become, lion, tiger, giraffe or monkey.

It is dawn as you venture onto the forest path. You have a bind rune of protection around your neck, nothing can harm you. The sun is coming up as the moon disappears through the trees, melting away the early mist. It is a magical time, not night and not yet day. The veil between the worlds is thin. It rained earlier and the water drips rhythmically through the branched canopy overhead, splashing on your face, refreshing you. Deep among the trees and foliage you see movement. A stag stands there. Squirrels run up and down the tree trunks as they begin their forage for nuts.

Something buzzes past your ear. It is a large bumblebee, and it settles on the petals of a wood anemone chasing away a butterfly. You hear a growl and something crashes through the trees. A wild pig runs across your path, it freezes for a moment and looks at you with fear on its face before running off into the dense undergrowth. You hesitate, touching your bind rune; you wait until the growling stops and walk on.

In the undergrowth you see three baby wolf cubs wrestling with each other. You stop to watch until mother-wolf appears and you quickly move on to show her you mean no harm. Further along the path there is a clearing and some wild ponies graze.

Continue in this way until you meet an animal that has direct contact with you. If nothing does then continue along the path until you reach a cove. You can now smell and taste the saltiness of the sea. On the horizon you see the sun rising and the water of the estuary glitters. It will be a calm day. You hear a great whoosh as a heron takes off to the side of you, its powerful beating wings startling you for a moment.

Seagulls dart in and out of the gentle waves catching their breakfast and screeching to warn other birds away. You see something in the water, a dolphin or seal. Soon others join it. Sensing you, they come close to the waters edge. You sit on the sand close to the trees and wait and watch the magnificent sunrise.

You should take at least 20 minutes for this exercise. Take time to recover after it. Ponder on what you saw as it could be more significant than you realize. Do not worry if you do not meet or connect with your fetch immediately. Keep trying the exercise and eventually you will have results.

Chapter 6

Making, Purifying and Empowering

Making Runes

We now come to how to make your own runes and how to cleanse them and empower them. The following instructions are for stones or pebbles only.

To find your stones, you can look on beaches, by rivers or on the land. You can also buy pebbles, stones, and crystals but this does not carry the same satisfaction, as by seeking your own you make a more instant personal connection. If you buy them and paint the symbols on with a paint that has to be baked, then be cautious as some bought pebbles fade and look strange when baked. Crystals fair better when subjected to heat. If you wish, you can apply varnish to the rune symbols only, to help preserve them.

My pebbles came from a river bank (I only collected exactly what I needed), and I used red ink to inscribe them and did not add any varnish and have had the same set for many years already without problems. I much prefer to not cover the entire surface of the stone or wood with varnish, as for me it cuts off or reduces the natural power of the material.

Red is the traditional color for staining, and it is thought that perhaps blood was used. Some thoughts are that this was symbolic of blood rather than actual blood. I would not suggest following the advice occasionally given, of staining with menstrual blood (I can feel some of you cringing at this). Menstrual blood is a powerful archetypal symbol but has both positive and negative aspects. We often add negative character-istics to menstruation ourselves just by calling it a nuisance, or "the curse", or just by sighing when we have a period because of the associated pain or heavier than normal flow. We sometimes even view it as unclean or messy. Of course we also view it as positive and we receive relief from menstrual flow, and of course it also points to fertility and the end of one cycle and the beginning of another.

Again cutting yourself to achieve a good blood supply is also not advisable or necessary and you could injure or scar yourself.

I use indelible red pen (only kept for this purpose) to mark the rune symbols on my stones. Normal ink, paint or natural dyes are other alternatives. If you find red is not suitable for the material, then I would suggest gold (associated with the sun) or perhaps silver (associated with the moon). Bought crystal runes sets are most often inscribed with gold.

Making Wooden Runes

To begin with, you will need to find some suitable wood. You could go to a D.I.Y. store and buy some wood or use a wooden broom handle. However, I recommend you go out and find some windfall wood.

Remember that the runes were cut from a fruit-bearing tree. This could mean any type of fruit, such as apple, pear, or walnut. Wood from any one of these and more will be ideal. There are other trees that bear fruit even though inedible. One of the sacred trees is a good idea, and these include oak, alder, ash, hazel, and holly. Otherwise try the wood of any sacred tree which does not bear fruit, such as the willow. Failing that, do not would not worry too much as for me all trees are magical and sacred, and any suitable windfall branch will be fine.

Some trees, such as some apple trees will not have a suitable branch as often they are rather crooked and gnarled. And you might find hard wood such as oak rather difficult to cut. Whichever wood you choose and even if you not even know what sort of wood it is, a good straight branch of about 30 cm or (12 inches), or one with just one or two curves (but it will need to be longer), is ideal. I would suggest finding a longer piece or more than one piece to allow for mistakes.

Going for a walk in woods or the park after a windy or stormy day, is part of the process of making your runes, and adds to the personal connection. If you can see the tree from whence the branch came, then thank it by pouring some water at the base or putting an offering of crystals or flowers in its branches. Put you hand on the tree and whisper your words of thanks, or of course a tree hug is beneficial to you to and connects you to the power of the tree.

You need to let your wood dry and season before use. If you wish you can smooth the surface of the back and front with sandpaper, but leave the edges with their natural look and with the bark intact if you prefer. This can peel off; however my wand which is made of willow has never peeled.

You can buy an electrical pyrograph (wood burning tool) from a do-it-yourself, craft or hobby shop, or from the internet. With this you burn the rune symbols onto the wood. I have a carving tool actually bought from a supermarket. It has tiny attachments for smoothing and polishing. You can do the burning or carving within a ritual or Sacred Circle. Then at the same time you can stain the runes with red paint or ink, or you can leave them as they are.

You can polish, varnish, or wax them then and wait with cleansing and empowering until the next day in a second ritual. Or you can make the runes without using a ritual or Circle and only use the ritual for cleansing and empowering. Experiment first with odd pieces of wood and see what works best. There are no hard and fast rules.

A note on varnishing; the wood will get dirty and lose its color, as wood is porous. However, although my views may not correspond with those of others, I have mentioned before that I do not like to cover the whole surface of the wood. An idea might be to let the edges stay free from varnish, and perhaps waxing or polishing is the better option.

Buying Runes

For some reason, it might not be practical to make your own runes, or it could be that this is beyond your capability at the present time. In that case it is perfectly all right to buy them. Also you might have received yours as a present and already have a connection with them.

You can buy runes in a variety of materials, some which can prove rather expensive. Crystals are perhaps the least expensive. Avoid tiles of man-made material such as plastic as the runes should be made of natural materials. To personalize them, you can follow the instructions for cleansing and empowering.

Making a Rune Bag

Now you have the materials for your runes, you will need a bag to keep them in. You can of course buy one, but ensure it is of natural material not synthetic. For making one you can use leather (as would have been the material used in past times), cotton, linen, Hessian (for wooden runes), silk, or cotton velvet. Sew up the bottom and sides and make a wide hem at the top. Tie or thread it with leather cord, string or silk ribbon. If your runes came with a synthetic bag, then make a new one. Ensure you make it big enough to accommodate your runes and your rune casting cloth.

A Sacred and Protective Circle

Part of the preparation of inscribing, purifying and empowering can be to cast a protective or Sacred Circle. It is up to you whether you choose to cast one or not, but I would like to give you the option as it helps in making the runes become personal and special to you.

The reasons for casting a Circle are valid. A Circle is a sphere or globe in which you perform magical work and meditations and is commonly called a Sacred Space. A Circle is protective and concentrates and contains the power and energy within it. The Circle is a symbol of unity, infinity, the cycles of life, death and rebirth, and the Self.

How Do I Cast a Sacred Circle?

You can cast the Circle in a number of ways. One of the easiest ways is to visualize a sphere of white or blue light forming around you and spreading out in a large circle. Or you can draw a Circle with salt.

You can if you wish ground and center yourself before the ritual. This should preferably be done out of doors and in your bare feet. If this is not possible then do it indoors. With great concentration, imagine all negative energies seeping out of you, down your body and out through the bottom of your feet and into the ground. Then imagine positive energies coming from the earth and up through your body. You should feel refreshed and ready to work. You can repeat it after you finish. Otherwise you can cleanse yourself by having a ritual bath. You can add lavender (oil is fine too) and/or sea salt to the water. When you have finished pull out the plug but stay in the bath and let all your negativities run out of you with the bath water. If you do not have a bath, then rub yourself with the salt or lavender (diluted essential oil is fine) and then shower it away.

This ritual is also useful for cleansing yourself of all negativities, which is sometimes required at the end of a relationship or bad phase in your life, to aid you in a new start.

Casting a Simple Circle

Place your altar in the north of the Circle as this corresponds with the Northern Mysteries, and include this in your Circle. You can estimate this by the position of the sun, if your garden or yard is south facing, then you know that north is at the front of the house.

Otherwise look to see where the sun is at midday as this will be south.

Your Circle need only be big enough to hold you, you equipment, and your work table or altar. You should see the Circle as a globe, which is all around you, above and below. Take your time with this and concentrate.

If you wish to purify the space first, sprinkle it with ground frankincense or lavender, and leave for a while before sweeping with a clean broom or small brush. If you do not have one, then leave the cleansing material in place, and clean it up later.

Begin by walking around the Circle from north to north with your index finger or rune wand if you have made one. You can read how make a rune wand in Chapter 8.

The standard way is then to Sprinkle the perimeter of the Circle space clockwise with salt or preferably salt mixed with water starting in the north. Follow it around again with a lit incense stick and then a third time with a candle from your table. These represent the four elements and use the magical three-times-fold. The salt and water represent the elements *Earth* and *Water*, the incense *Air*, and the candle *Fire*. Earth is in the north, water, in the west, air in the east, and fire in the south of the Circle. A candle of appropriate colors can be placed at the four compass points, green (or brown) in the north, blue in the west, yellow in the east, and red in the south.

However, and to keep more to what is appropriate, you can incorporate the elements of the runes, *Earth, Water, Ice, Air* and *Fire*. In this case it is usual to place the earth in the center (as with Midgard), water in the west, ice in the north, air in the east, and fire in the south.

Then you can place something of the element represented at each compass point. I would suggest salt at the earth point, water in the west, an ice-cube in the north, incense in the east, and a red candle in the south. You can then go on to use these items to cleanse your runes.

To cast this Circle place all the items clockwise at their appropriate points starting at the north and ending at the center. Cast the Circle with your rune wand or finger, from north to north and walking around the Circle clockwise. You can complete a three times Circle casting by walking around a third time with incense.

A Basic Circle

If you wish something even simpler you can just use the salt, moving clockwise around and leave it at that. If you keep a brush in the Circle you can then close it by sweeping it all way anti-clockwise. But please still visualize yourself in a globe.

The Integrity of the Circle

To keep the integrity of the Circle, do not leave it once it is cast. If it is at all necessary to leave the Circle then cut a doorway clockwise (deosil) with a finger and close it behind you anti-clockwise (widdershins), and re-enter in the same way. This is traditionally done in the north-east. Cats and other animals can come and go safely through the walls of the Circle.

Banishing or Closing the Circle

To close the Circle, simply use your finger as a pointer or your rune wand. With your arm stretched out, walk around the Circle anti-clockwise. You can also declare the Circle closed and banished and all energies released.

Inscribing, Purifying and Empowering

Preparation

Have a look at each rune symbol aett by aett, and choose the stones or wood you would like for each symbol. Otherwise close your eyes and choose one from the bag either at random or by feeling around until you come to a stone or piece of wood that suggests itself to that particular rune symbol. Lay them out in order, in three rows of eight.

I suggest you inscribe and empower your runes on a full moon or during the waxing phase, when the forces of nature are at their most powerful.

What you will need

An altar or work table (this can be a coffee table, a bedside table, an upturned cardboard box covered with a cloth, or indeed anything you can use to work on. If you can keep it expressly for this purpose and for spell work that would be ideal).

Cleansing incense such as Frankincense resin

(If you can't obtain the above, use sticks or cones)

Heatproof container

Incense charcoal (available from New-age shops or internet)

Matches or lighter

Soft music, such as meditation music

Salt, water, an ice-cube, incense stick or cone, and a red candle (if you wish to cast a Sacred Circle and depending on the type of circle you decide to cast)

2 Altar candles

Rune wand if you have one

I would recommend inscribing, empowering, and cleansing at the same time, so prepare your room. Light candles, and incense, play relaxing music. Prepare your altar with your incense that you wish to use for the cleansing. Below is a simple circle cast for those who wish to try this. This is especially relevant to those who prefer to use a Sacred Circle in magical workings.

Inscribing

Take the first rune *Fehu*. Hold it in your hand and read or think about the meaning of it. Then inscribe the symbol with the chosen material, do this with each rune. Let them dry for a few minutes.

For wooden runes, presuming they are already cut, burn or

carve the symbols. If you have already done this then go onto the next section.

Purifying or Cleansing

Why should we purify or cleanse the runes? Well, while making your runes, it could be that others have handled them, or they have been subjected to all sorts of outside influences or negativities, which would be prudent to remove. Moreover, to spiritually cleanse the runes is part of the process of forming a personal connection with them.

This ritual incorporates the cleansing power of the elements. You will need *salt, incense, water, a red candle, and an ice-cube.* You can cleanse all of the runes in one go or one at a time as you think fit.

"A higher power" can be a god or goddess preferably from the Northern Pantheon especially the father of the runes, Odin. Otherwise light elves from the realms of Yggdrasil would be suitable. If you feel uncomfortable with this then use the universal energies. "Universal energies" are just that, the energies of the universe. You can substitute this for the powers of nature.

The chant below presumes you have gone for the runic elements Circle.

Pass the rune or runes over the ice three times and chant:
In the name of (the higher power or universal energies), and by the power of Ice, I eradicate all negativity from these runes and so purify them.

Pass the rune or runes through the cleansing incense three times and chant:
In the name of (the higher power or universal energies), and by the power of Air, I eradicate all negativity from these runes and so purify them.

Pass the rune or runes through the flame of a candle and chant:
In the name of (the higher power or universal energies), and by the power

of Fire, I eradicate all negativity from these runes and so purify them.

Sprinkle the rune or runes with water and chant:
In the name of (the higher power or universal energies), and by the power of Water, I eradicate all negativity from these runes and so purify them

Sprinkle the rune or runes with salt and chant:
In the name of (the higher power or universal energies), and by the power of Earth, I eradicate all negativity from these runes and so purify them.

You can alter the chant if you wish.

Empowering

Empowering or charging your runes will activate them. We do this by imbuing them with magical energy, which prepares them for both divining and magic.

The calls to the god or goddess represent a higher power. With Frey and Freyja we are actually calling on the magical or sacred forces of nature, and to Odin, to magical forces of communication and divinatory power. I have used Freyja here to provide a chant for both the god and goddess. You can use *chant one* or even both.

You can of course devise your own ritual and chants to suit your own beliefs.

Before you start ensure you have a small sample of each element in front of you. Also make sure you have the list of runes with their associated elements on the altar.

Facing north, take a single rune in one hand, (starting with *Fehu*), and think of the meaning. Pass it through the red candle flame and then the incense three times each. With your other hand, and visualizing a blue light coming from the end of your forefinger or use your rune wand, draw the rune symbol in the air in front of you and read the chant, which you can lay on your work table or altar. Continue (in the correct order) until you have empowered all of the runes, using the correct associated element or elements.

Oh Freyja, lady beautiful, mistress of magic, goddess of love, devotion, fertility, and powers of nature, hail and welcome to this Sacred Space. I ask you to create a bond between myself and this rune (name rune) and bring forth the power within, in accordance with the wisdom and insight of the ancient ways of the Runemasters.

Oh Odin, wise father, shaman and teacher, god of communication and magic, hail and welcome to this Sacred Space. I ask you to create a bond between myself and this rune (name rune) and bring forth the power within, in accordance with the wisdom and insight of the ancient ways of the Runemasters.

Repeat with each rune. With this ritual you create a personal bond with the rune.

An alternative way of empowering the runes would be to take them to a sacred and ancient place and perform the ritual or devise one of your own. As an addition, I took my runes to the stone circle at Avebury in Wiltshire, England.

You can also bathe your runes in moonlight to further empower them. This is handy if you have a skylight. Look and see if the moon shines through it. Wait until the moon is full, and then place the runes on the floor in the moonlight. You can find out in the previous days at what time the moon appears and where the light falls. Another alternative would be to place the runes in sunlight which also empowers them and depending on your preference, or do both.

Chapter 7

Casting and Reading

When reading the runes, take into account which runes in the casting come from which particular aett.

In the *Tacitus Casting* (see below), the first or "past" rune could come from Frey/Freyja's aett, and the other two from Hagal's. Look to what I say about each aett and think how this would affect your reading. Looking at the first rune which is from Frey/Freyja's aett, it could be that when you think about it events have gone your way up until the present moment and without much effort. The fact that the other two runes are from Hagal's aett possibly means that from now on times will be more difficult or that you have to work harder to get the same results. Intuition will guide you in this and as you become experienced you will find it easier.

In a *Circle Casting*, this is done anyway in the reading; you look to where the runes lie in conjunction with each other, and in which realm they lay. In an Yggdrasil Reading, it is also explained. In a *One-Rune* reading the aett the rune belongs to, should be looked at in conjunction with the rune.

With any reading there are no hard and fast rules. We do not really know exactly how the runes were used apart from writings from Tacitus and others, fragmented mythology, medieval writings and later interpretations. As long as you have belief in your methods, this is what really counts. All the ways of casting are just a guide. You will eventually discover what works for you.

A Note on the Northern Traditions and other such revivals

It is impossible to use the runes exactly the way they were used by the Nordic and Germanic peoples around two thousand years ago, as we do not know their exact practices. We can only draw on the sources available to us, from mythology, historical finds, and from later historians.

With Pagan revivals of any type, such as the Northern Traditions, Wicca, and Celtic, you always will have people declaring that their practices came from age-old secret traditions, covens, or guilds, and passed down through their families or by other means and that they cannot reveal their sources. I have seen this in books and on the internet. Yet, when you look at their practices, they are clearly modern with information easily available in books and indeed on the internet. In these cases it is always the case that evidence is never offered, and usually excused by the statement "It's a secret and no one is allowed to see the literature", or "It's word of mouth". We cannot say for sure that there are never some cases where this is true but at the least they will produce original material. However, I have never come across such people up unto the present time. Unfortunately, what is usually the case is that the age-old veil of secrecy is hidden behind, to perhaps add an authenticity and a convincing case for their book, or for their organization. Why is not always clear, perhaps insecurity, perhaps to defraud the general public (in this case money is sometimes requested).

It is common knowledge now, chiefly through later admissions or thorough research by respected researches such as Prof. Ronald Hutton author of *Triumph of the Moon,* and other books on Pagan practices that Wicca for instance is the modern invention of Gerald Gardner. Gardner gained his ideas from the work of others, from folklore and secret societies like the *Freemasons* and the *Hermetic Order of the Golden Dawn,* and some which was later admitted to be the work of his friend and associate Doreen Valiente. This tradition of inventing a system of magical and spiritual practice from ancient sources continues to this day.

On the other hand we have the faithful Reconstructionists of pathways such as Northern and Celtic. Many, but by no means all, who follow these pathways stay rigidly with the culture studied with no flexibility and are stuck with a limiting form of "political correctness" and are often called "purists". Some label others with names such as "fluffies" who dare think or practice otherwise. Yet religions change over the centuries and so do cultures. Aspects of some cultures appear in others having been introduced by liberal or perhaps lateral thinkers. How can a past practice be truly authenticated when we have not lived in those times, have only limited knowledge provided by historical sources influenced by other religions and recorded by man who is not infallible, and we are not ourselves omnipresent or omnipotent?

We live in modern times and have the benefit of more knowledge and understanding of the world in which we live, and furthermore have many resources and much material at our disposal than were available to our ancestors. No matter how we use the runes we can be sure that it will be radically different from the way they were used in the past. We really cannot restore an exact ancient culture of runelore.

I prefer an honest approach. For me there is nothing wrong with mixing all that we have learned from the scholars and adding our own ideas we have found work very well, while keeping to the essence of that particular tradition. It is perfectly valid as long as we know that it works for us and it is only natural to wish to share it with others. I advise people to find there own way, perhaps after looking at the ideas of others, by widely reading, and using what they believe is right and fits with their own intuitive feelings. What we need to keep in mind is not to be gullible about the origins of some modern reconstructions, but at the same time not to be too cynical and restrictive concerning modern methods. We cannot go back and live in the past; we live in the here and now. As long as your intention is honorable and you are not being flippant then this is what matters.

This brings me to the next subject of casting and how we approach this in modern times. Perhaps we should think about how things will have changed many years into the future. Who would have thought just thirty years ago that we would be doing things we had only previously seen in futuristic programs and films. We now speak to people face to face on mobile or cell phones, and carry around computers on which we can speak with people all over the world. We now have knowledge of distant planets and solar systems and men have landed on the moon. Only a few hundred years ago people thought the earth was flat. We also have a deeper understanding of human psychology and of the mysteries of the world.

So in the future how will things have changed again? Will more people have discovered spiritual enlightenment? Many people now seek spiritual enlightenment, and many more are finding it. Moreover, we are learning to use the parts of the psyche previously neglected. So who knows how we will evolve in the future.

Over the centuries traditions did not stay static but changed with the times and the people. Someone at sometime invented ways of casting for instance, or devised spells, and others followed. Staying with just one way would be restricting and would prevent us from growing. For instance the *Tacitus Casting* is three runes. This is the casting I prefer and use the most as it works well for me but I expand it (up to) a nine rune casting as (for me) it is more useful. I also treat one rune each as the past, present and future, which fits nicely with the attributes of the Norns. My *Yggdrasil Reading* it is based on Yggdrasil cosmology (naturally), and mixed with the Norse human cosmology, with elements of modern psychology.

Personally, I try to be faithful to the spirit of the runes and always try to devise something that fits with them. I generally avoid methods that were devised for other forms of divination. However, just because I do not use them, it does not mean that you should not. And I am certainly "guilty" of employing other non-traditional methods concerning the runes. However, I embrace the core knowledge of Norse mythology and understanding of rune origins, and in doing so I consider my connection to the runes to be an honest one.

So to sum up, I would suggest that perhaps we should keep an open mind and not place too many restrictions on ourselves and on the runes. Try not to get too one-track-minded and do not let others cause you to feel guilty about moving with the times. So go ahead and use the knowledge you have gained about the runes, your talents, personal beliefs, and along with perhaps any personal magical knowledge you have at your disposal, and find what works for you. There are hidden secrets to discover, so jump right in, delve around, and seek out some truths of your own.

Casting and Reading

For casting I always cast onto a cloth. I see the runes as somehow sacred and casting them directly onto a floor or table, to me seems wrong. In ancient times, a white cloth was used. We know this from the Roman historian Tacitus, who mentions it in his writings. So that is what I prefer to use. If you want to use a cloth, and I would recommend you do, wash it and keep it exclusively for casting. Ensure it is made of cotton or linen. You can buy this quite cheaply at a market or look for oddments and simply hem it. Keep it clean and washed.

Concerning the divination of the runes, I prefer to use the overall term of "casting" or "castings" and prefer the term "layout" to "spread", I also use "reading".

Below are my suggestions for rune castings.

The Tacitus Casting Method

This method of casting is based on the description by Tacitus, the first century ce. Roman historian, and you can call on the gods/goddesses or your chosen higher power to assist in the interpretation if you wish. You will need your large cloth. Set the scene if you are able. I use candles and burn herbal incense as described in the visualization exercises. Bought incense can also be used. You will find the principles of this way of casting easier to grasp.

Sit facing north and if you are reading for someone then that person should sit opposite you facing south. I like to use a low stool for this. If the reading is just for you, then sit facing north. You can find out where north is by buying a compass from a camping shop. Otherwise, if you do not know this already, wait until a sunny day and see where the sun is at midday and choose the opposite direction. In the room you have chosen to do your readings, choose a focal point to approximately give you north, such as the corner of the doorway, the middle of a wall, a picture on the wall, or a piece of furniture, and remember it for the future.

Think about the question(s) to be asked. Take the runes in your power hand (the one you write with), or if this is not possible in both hands, and after calling on the gods/goddesses, or the powers of the universe (I call on the Norns - Urd, Verdandi, and Skuld and ask them to assist me in my reading and interpretation of the runes), throw them onto your large white cloth.

Form the particular question in your mind and choose three runes one at a time. Lay them across a clear part of the cloth and read them. Alternatively, read each as you choose it and lay it down on the cloth for cross reference, and read the next one. Instead of using the same cloth for laying them out, especially if your cloth is on the small side, you can buy a large man's handkerchief and lay it next to your casting cloth to lay the runes upon after choosing, so they do not get confused with the runes you have cast. Then look at the three runes in conjunction with each other.

This rune reading takes you about three to six months into the future though the events can happen sooner than that. I see the first rune as being the past that has led up to the present, the second rune as being the present into the near future, (up to three months), and the third rune is the near future onwards (up to six months). I do not know why it works like this. I have worked out from my own feedback on present and following events and that of others I have read for. It might work differently for you so keep a rune diary.

If the answers the runes give you throw up more queries then choose three more runes asking another *connected* question. You can do this up until you have nine runes. You can then cross-reference the runes. Stop at this point and make a fresh cast if necessary repeating the procedure. You will find at some point there is nothing more to be asked or you will feel the reading should stop. Strangely, I always find that people I read for also do this. They suddenly feel enough has been asked, and I have never had to suggest to someone that we should stop.

A word of advice is to be wary about asking questions about health. If a future crisis does show in some way, *waiting to find out what it will be is not very nice. So take heed.*

A One-Rune or Advice Rune reading

This is an easier one. We take the bag of runes in one hand and consider the question we need to ask, but word it carefully. Choose one rune with your power hand (the hand you write with). Decide beforehand if a positive rune is going to be *yes* and a negative rune *no*, or vice versa. I prefer to ask a direct question such as, "Will I be able to go on holiday this year?" then if a rune comes out such as *Raidho* then I will be sure to travel, but if *Isa* turns up, then perhaps circumstances will prevent it. You can also choose a rune like this as a daily guide, or a rune for strength or to advise you in times of need.

Casting onto Circles

This is another way to cast the runes using three ever increasing circles embroidered or drawn on a cloth. You take three runes at a time from the bag again with your power hand, and cast them together onto the cloth. You can cast three, six, or nine, runes. This reading can help you in decision-making. However, leave this way of casting until you become more familiar with the runes as it is more difficult to comprehend.

There are three realms. Decide what the circles represent. For instance, for me the inner one is *Kenaz*, the realm of the emotions and how the situation is or might affect us, the middle circle is *Mannaz*, the earthly realm of practical matters and what we need to do, and the outer circle is *Nauthiz* the realm of the hidden or that which we need to face up to.

As you can see each circle relates to an aett. The inner circle of *Kenaz* is related to Frey/Freyja. The middle circle of *Mannaz* is related to Tyr. The outer circle of *Nauthiz* is related to Hagal.

If runes fall outside the outer circle you could decide it means that these things should not be taken into consideration. Decide beforehand if this is so. I use the runes falling on the outer edges of the cloth (which is square) as advice runes.

Look to see how many runes fall into each realm as this could be significant. If more runes fall into the inner realm of *Kenaz*, then the problem could be affecting you personally more than you think. If more fall into the middle realm of Tyr for instance then you will have concentrate on practical matters and look for help and guidance in the matter. If more runes fall into the outer realm of *Nauthiz*, then you really need to decide on what is essential and the actions that you need to follow.

For instance, if you have a financial problem and *Uruz* falls into the realm of *Kenaz*/Frey-Freyja, then you do have the strength to help yourself through the situation, especially as it fell into its related circle (of Frey). You can be assured of assistance from others, and luck will come your way.

If *Ansuz* falls into the realm of *Mannaz*/Tyr, then practical help in the way of communication is required to solve the problem, and you perhaps need to address the people involved directly or ask for assistance in working something out. Or talk to someone in an official capacity. *Ansuz* actually fell into the unrelated circle (of Tyr), but it does bring a certain amount of good fortune into the situation, and you should be able to discover a satisfactory solution.

Isa in the realm of *Nauthiz*/Hagal possibly means that you have ignored the situation too long and the time has come to do what is necessary to improve things. Again *Isa* fell into its related circle (of Hagal), so use your intuition as guidance through tough times.

Remember to look at all the runes in conjunction with one another, as advice will be forthcoming.

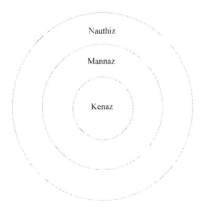

The Circles

Yggdrasil Reading (a more advanced reading)

The Yggdrasil reading is particularly useful for a problem which is plaguing us. We can find out what influences are affecting us from solving this problem and see where we are going wrong. We can also ask for advice to help us in the solving of this problem.

The three bottom runes of the underworld are concerned with what has caused the problem and help us to face what we might be ignoring. In this realm we should learn to face up to our faults (see "Shadow" in the Glossary of the Psyche), and what has led us into our present situation. Revealed in this realm are glimmers of ways to extricate ourselves from the situation or come to terms with it. However, we are possibly not picking up the signals of this, owing to panic or despair.

The three middle runes of the earthly realms are the past, present, and likely outcome of the problem. They also represent what is obvious to us. Here we need to attend to the practical side of the problem. We need to use our heads rather than our hearts.

The three higher runes are in the spiritual realms and offer help and advice. They are protective and provide luck. They can send us messages of guidance from the spiritual world or from the unconscious. Below is a guide to Yggdrasil reading and I based this on the Norse cosmology (Yggdrasil) and human cosmology as discussed in Chapter 5.

<pre>
    Spiritual   Help
    Realms   9   Advice
       8   7

                  5

    Earthly   Past
    Realms   4   6   Present
                           future

                  1

       2   3
  Underworld   The Problem
</pre>

Yggdrasil Reading

Reading from the bottom, places 1, 2, and 3, are from the darker realms. This is where the problem lies. We need to lift ourselves out of this realm to solve the problem. Hagal will help us with this.

Places 4, 5, and 6, are from the realm of humankind. Here we can find out how the past and present are affecting the future and the status of affairs. Tyr will guide us in this.

Places 7, 8, and 9, are in the higher realms. We can from here take spiritual advice and also practical advice. We can find out the likely outcome of the problem. Frey/Freyja will help us in this.

Below is a guide to each position and how to proceed.

1. We have here at the root of the tree, the problem itself and its severity. We can see from this how difficult it will be to find a solution.

2. Here is what hinders us from moving forward, most probably coming from within ourselves, and possibly hidden. We need to look at our personal faults or shadow side.

3. Here are ideas coming from within that will contribute to a solution to the problem (and also what we need to take into consideration).

4. Here are past influences (that have contributed to the problem), and that which we cannot change (Orlog).

5. Here lie present influences. We can help ourselves by changing the patterns (in 4) that keeps causing situation and problems. We also have here practical advice to guide us in this. Someone may come into our lives to give us advice.

6. Here is what the future holds if we leave things as they are. It might be that we do not need to do anything. However, a negative rune here perhaps shows that we do need to act.

7. Here is protection and luck gifted to us spiritually or from within ourselves. We should always be optimistic and here we might discover a light at the end of the tunnel.

8. Here lies the advice from the inner world (spiritual advice that we can find within ourselves). It is also outer spiritual help. We will receive messages to assist us through this rune.

9. Here lies the likely outcome of the problem if we follow the advice given.

Cast your runes onto your cloth, then after asking for help from above, either close your eyes or look upwards before choosing nine runes one at a time and place them in the above positions. Make sure you keep your eyes from drifting towards the runes as you choose each one. Alternatively, choose runes direct from the bag one at a time.

When you have read all the runes, you can have another look to see how the runes relate to each other. In the realm of humankind for instance, we can look to see what obvious things have helped contribute to the problem. We look to ourselves in this. Do any of Tyr's runes sit in this realm? If they do then these are of particular significance. If the runes of Frey/Freyja sit here then it is of less significance but means that we are possibly relying on the problem to sort itself out rather than helping to solve it our selves, and if the runes of Hagal sit here, then we might have missed something that can help or direct us in solving the problem.

If runes from Frey/Freyja sit in the darker realms, then it might be that things are not as bad as we thought. If the runes of Hagal sit in here then the problem is a little more difficult to solve, however, Hagal is here to help. If the runes of Tyr fall here, then look for specific direction.

Going to the higher realms, if we find runes of Frey/Freyja here we can be assured of a good outcome to the problem. If we find the runes of Hagal here, it will depend on what they are. It could be that the problem will take time resolve, or that runes of protection or optimism will encourage us. If the runes of Tyr fall here then we should with help, either practical or spiritual, be able to solve the problem.

This way of casting is more complicated, so I would suggest using it after you gain more experience. Below I have added an example to help you understand it.

Sample Reading

The question asked is a financial one. Couple A has had major financial problems. After much hard work and outside help, following previous advice from the runes, they feel they are getting somewhere. However, will the end results be worth it?

This is the layout of the runes chosen.

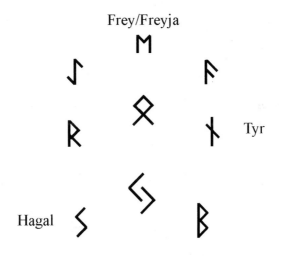

Sample Yggdrasil Reading

A quick glance tells me that in general this is a positive reading. The realms of the unconscious and underworld reveal positive aspects.

Jera the season, in position 1, brings harvest to the needy. This is a Hagal rune so significant in that positive forces are at work. Life is difficult and hard work is the key. And hard work has indeed paid off and Couple A is waiting to reap the benefits of their labors. Patience was exercised and my intuition tells me that the Couple A is feeling a little more hopeful. This is now discussed with them, giving them a chance to open up and perhaps tell me some of the problems they have had and yet persevered with.

Sowilo the sun in position 2 tells me that optimism and confidence have not been easily forthcoming. As another Hagal rune positive forces are again at work here. Couple A tends to be pessimistic. I discuss this with them. They tell me that they found it hard to be optimistic as everything was so overwhelming. However, with the outside help, they are now beginning to see the light at the end of the tunnel. I tell them that they need to keep hopeful and optimistic. Positive thoughts going out attract positive events back. *Sowilo* is there as their guiding light, and will lead them to safe harbor. They agree and appear to be heartened by this.

Berkano in position 3 tells me that the couple has plans in place to help them through the bad times. This is a rune of Tyr and points Couple A in the right direction. I have a thought here that they perhaps have the ability to start a new project which will lift their spirits and eventually contribute to their income. However, my intuition tells me that they already have a new project in mind or have perhaps started one. They look surprised and tell me that this indeed is correct. They decided to use their talents to engage in a new project which they both enjoy and are rather excited about. It will take time and it will be slow going to start with. However, they have their doubts about it and worry it will not come to anything.

I again point out their pessimistic natures. Sometimes when things keep going wrong we begin to think that this is our lot. However, through life everyone has good and bad times. Again keeping positive is the key. The bad times will pass. I advise them to take it one step at a time and nurture the project and eventually they will see the results. They should have more faith in themselves. A short while ago they did not think they would get through their present troubles.

As we move into the earthly and practical realms, a first glance tells me what the past problem was and that they should be careful not to fall into the same trap.

Raidho in position 4 as their Orlog, or what in the past has contributed to their problem, reveals that this to be constant change and moving of home, areas, and jobs. As a rune of Frey within Tyr what is considered here is that the emotional part of Couple A has ruled over the thinking part. On the one hand constant change has provided much excitement, but on the other there has been no stability in their home life. This is a couple who are easily bored, and they tell me that as they both agree on everything, it is difficult to make informed decisions. If one of them had preferred safety and security it would probably have made a difference. This is the reason why they have decided to stay put and build a more stable life and work on the new project which will provide them with something positive and exciting to do. I advised them that this is perhaps the right thing to do, especially taking into consideration the next rune.

Othala in position 5 reveals that couple a have a life with more stability, especially as *Othala* lies in its own realm. The couple has made a home and they are managing at present to resist the urge to move. Everything in their lives has elements of stability, their home and jobs, and also within friendships. They feel at home, but they need to preserve it.

However, *Nauthiz* in position 6 reveals problems for the future. Couple A should not panic if things do not go as well as they thought they would. They need to prioritize and Tyr will help them with this. Overspending is a danger and new projects take time to blossom. Relying on themselves more and using their own initiative and common sense will guide them through. This is a danger time and a move will be even harder to resist, but if they persevere they will win through. Everyone goes through troubling and harder periods; it is a part of life.

In position 7 is *Eihwaz* is in itself a spiritual and protective rune. It brings luck for Couple A's new projects and excellent general protection. It advises them to put the past behind them and to embrace the new life that is offered to them. This is not the easiest of times for them, but time will bring its rewards. A new cycle of life is beginning for them and they should have faith in themselves.

Ansuz in position 8 a rune of Frey in the realm of Frey, brings it own special rewards. Odin himself offers spiritual assistance. Good powers of communication are theirs to use and will benefit them. The power is strong and they have good control of the situation. The help and support they are receiving will continue, and they can ask for more spiritual help as they need it.

Finally in position 9 is *Ehwaz*. This couple's sense of adventure tended to rule over everything else, including security, and got them into some difficulties. They were already seeing that they needed to look at what they must do and to stick with it. Deep down they knew they were doing the right thing now, now matter how much the struggle. But *Ehwaz* brings them some hope and shows them to be good partners with a strong relationship. This will continue and nothing can shake this couple's love and commitment to each other.

Couple A is on a security building journey. And as *Ehwaz* the horse also brings comfort to the restless, affairs will not stay static and they can expect good progress. They will continue to move forward with their lives satisfying the restlessness that they both have inside them. Projects will be successful and they have the energy to see them through. This will in turn prevent boredom from setting in and they can look forward to an eventful and interesting life that will be forever on the move, whilst a secure base is maintained. *Ehwaz* ensures that some travel is in the offing, and I can see myself that this will be without them losing this newfound security.

Overall this is a very encouraging reading.

Chapter 8

Rune Magic

A twelfth I know: if I see in a tree
a corpse hanging from a halter
these spells I write and paint in runes
and the being descends and speaks.
(From *The Song of Spells, The Havamal*)

I have left this section until last for a reason. A "one size fits all" approach is not appropriate in rune magic. The runes have hidden powers, and you will need to have a good knowledge and understanding of them, not least that ever-important connection, before embarking on magical usage. It might appear that this section is filled with warnings, but this is necessary, as magic is a complicated business.

Runes none should ever carve
Who knows not how to read them

The above two lines comes from one of the Icelandic Sagas, *The Saga of Egil Skallagrimsson,* attributed to Snorri Sturluson and written somewhere in the thirteenth century. It comes from tales relating to the ninth and tenth centuries.

It tells of Egil who comes to eat at the house of Thorfinn. As he and his comrades sat to eat, Egil noticed a sick woman lying at the end of the hall. He asked about her and was told that it was Helga daughter of Thorfinn, and that she had a pining sickness. Egil asked if anything had been done for her, and was told that runes had been given by a landowner's son and since then she had become worse.

After he had eaten Egil went to the bed of Helga and spoke with her. He asked for her to be lifted onto fresh bedding. This was done, and Egil then searched the bed. He found a piece of whalebone inscribed with runes. Egil read them and then cut and scratched off the runes into the fire, and then he burned the whalebone. He asked for Helga's bedding to be hung out to air.

Egil engraved new runes and laid them in the bed where Helga now lay. She rapidly recovered and although weak felt well once more.

This tale is a warning not to use runes in healing or magic if you do not know them well. If you use the runes without knowing what you are really doing, they will still work as you see from the tale; however, not in the way you expect or want them to! So the lesson here is to be careful and know your runes.

Consequently in this section I am presuming that you know what you are doing, or you are reading this for when you are more experienced. What I have done here is to give simple examples of how the runes can be bound together for magical or healing purposes, and how this works. But before doing that I will explain a little about Norse magic and how magic works, to those who are new to it.

Seidhr

Seidhr is a form of ancient Norse magic principally performed by women. Although some men also practiced it, it was thought of as unmanly as the practitioner having moved into a trance state, became vulnerable to earthly dangers.

The goddess Freyja was a proficient practitioner of Seidhr magic, which was practiced by the Vanir. When Freyja joined the Aesir with her father Njord and her brother Frey, it is said that she passed her knowledge on to Odin.

Seidhr has a strong association with shamanism, in that the practitioner uses a trance state to perform magical work. The trance enables the practitioner through an altered state of consciousness to gain access to the astral plains. In this trance state, the practitioner can prophesize, divine the future, influence the weather, shape shift, influence the minds of others, and all manner of spell work and magical acts. The practitioner of Seidhr on their travel onto other plains meets with spirits and elementals to ask for assistance to carry out magical work. In the past, it is thought that some of this work was for negative purposes. Today the practitioner of Seidhr would only work with positive magic. Even in the past, the 18 rune charms (found in a full version of the *Havamal*), most if not all can be understood to be for positive magic.

Seidhr is said to be a dangerous form of magic, however, if properly taught and guided the novice should be perfectly safe. There are modern groups who specialize in Seidhr and it would be wise to join a reputable one if you are interested in this branch of magic.

Galdr

Galdr relates more to the ritual branch of magic discussed here, and particularly with rune magic. It involves chants, more often than not, poetic chants, and speaking aloud. When words and names are spoken aloud it brings more power. Many practitioners of magic prefer to use poetical chanting, as it has rhythm and is easier to remember. It also has a better sound to it; it is pleasing to the ears. For the same reason the chant can also be sung. However, many rune chants resemble those of meditation chants, and are popular with modern practitioners of rune magic.

Principles of Magic

How Does a Charm Work?

When you cast a spell or charm, you are purposely promoting change. This is done through altering physical reality (or matter) in a way that harmonizes with the power of your mind. It is in essence mind over matter but in a more agreeable or harmonizing way. So we use charms and spells to help create or change events in our own lives and that of others and achieve this through the power of will. It is connected with synchronicity in that it encourages the interconnection between mind and matter, or psychic and actual events.

The charm or spell is presented as a magical, spoken, or in the case of rune symbols, written formula, and performed within a ritual. The power of thought is of great importance for the workings of a charm. When we cast the charm or spell we tap into the invisible. Great concentration, visualization, and patience are required to make it effective.

People of different religions pray to their God. This might be for a soul, a cure for an illness, or help in a difficult situation and is often said within a ritual such as a mass or a prayer meeting, for instance candles might be lit, and incense burned, with joint prayers and chants said for extra effect. Charms and spells are very much the same. Some people invoke a goddess or god, or other spiritual beings, use candles, chants, and other items, while concentrating on the wish required.

You must have faith in the rune charm even if you are not totally sure how the magic works.

Ritual

Ritual helps our mindset. It is a discipline that helps us reach into the invisible. A ritual works symbolically as each movement represents something. Symbols work on a conscious and subconscious level. In the case of the charm the symbols work on both. However, ritual also reveals a mythic reality. What happens within the ritual is invisible (the altering of reality), a sort of sacred narrative working in the background, but of which the runecaster is conscious and believes in. Within the ritual we pass through different stages of the charm in order to create it. All the time we are focused on the goal of the charm and have a heightened awareness of what is happening, this also helps in summoning up the invisible energies that make it work.

Black and White Magic

Charms and Spells, positive and negative, have been around since ancient times and used in many cultures. It is often said that magic is black, white or grey. However, magic is neither positive nor negative, but neutral, and it is how you use it that makes it good or bad, positive or negative. All of the runes can be used for negative as well as positive magic.

However, a negative charm or spell does not necessarily translate as "evil" or "black". A binding spell is classed as negative as it is cast to prevent one person from harming another or others. It is up to the individual if they think this is in opposition to their personal ethics. A love charm or spell (in that one person is willed to love another and against what is natural) would be a negative one, and most people would agree that this type of charm should never be employed. We cannot force another to love us. Moreover, this would be a false love and not a real love and would not in the long run be beneficial to the recipient. This happened to Frey when he sent his servant Skirnir to woo Gerd, giving his magic sword to him as a reward. Skirnir accomplished his task with the use of magical runes. However the loss of his sword causes the downfall of Frey at Ragnarok. An alternative to a love spell would be a charm to get us noticed, or a general attraction charm.

Not every person believes in the law of karma, and some people do cast negative charms and spells as long as they are not meant intentionally to harm another, possibly for protection or to prevent harm being done.

Whatever you decide, you should not cast negative charms or spells without a lot of forethought over the possible conse-quences. If in doubt, avoid it. If you think it is negative, listen to yourself, it probably is. There is a fine line between what is right and what is wrong, but experience will help in the long run.

If someone asks you to write a charm, you can say no if you feel that it would take too much out of you, or if the problem is beyond your capabilities, or if you feel it is inappropriate. A charm is not the answer to every problem.

How is a charm put together?

Before going on to Bind Runes, I will explain how a charm or spell is put together. To demonstrate this I am going to use a simple sponge cake recipe.

Recipe

100g (4 oz) Self-raising flour
100g (4 oz) Butter
100g (4 oz) Caster sugar
2 eggs
Jam to fill

On their own these ingredients do not make a cake, but blend them together and they do. However, let me add something strange to the mix:
100g (4 oz) salt
6 tablespoons of vinegar

Perhaps I did not understand what the ingredients are, or I am a child who decided that to put anything in would be all right.

As you will agree this will not make a tasty sponge cake and the result will be inedible (well, I have never actually tried it!). The ingredients do not go together. They conflict, and do not harmonize or blend well.

However, let me instead add one large tablespoon of cocoa as an extra in ingredient instead, and in place of jam use chocolate butter cream to fill. These extra ingredients will enhance the cake; they will also change it from a jam sponge to a chocolate cake. If this is what I intended then in this case it is fine.

If I want to put some icing on this cake to further enhance it; again this is perfectly all right.

And so it is the same with a charm or spell. You cannot put ingredients in that conflict. You really need to know what the ingredients are that you are using, and ensure that they harmonize.

You can add extra ingredients to further enhance the charm, such as burn corresponding incense or candles. For instance, I would not use black candles for a success charm, but yellow (you will find a list of color correspondences at the end of the book). I am likely to use a citrine gemstone, not an obsidian (as it is more suitable for protection), and a suitable chant, and perform the whole thing at the time of the full moon (not a waning moon).

Consequently, you will see that it is important to get the correspondences right.

Principles of Rune Magic

When we are practicing rune magic it is well to remember the Havamal, and how I have described the construction of the runes. These lines are also appropriate in rune magic.

Knowest how one shall write, | knowest how one shall rede?
Knowest how one shall tint, | knowest how one makes trial?
Knowest how one shall ask, | knowest how one shall offer?
Knowest how one shall send, | knowest how one shall sacrifice?

The first two lines: *Knowest how one shall write, | knowest how one shall rede?* These lines will link to the writing or carving of the runes symbols (for us perhaps carving on wood, stone, or a candle or writing on paper) and knowing the runes well, before we even think about magic.

The second two lines: *Knowest how one shall tint, | knowest how one makes trial?* These lines will link to which color to write your rune symbols in, and how to construct the charm correctly.

The third two lines: *Knowest how one shall ask, | knowest how one shall offer?* These lines will refer to an evocation using magical incense to assist you in contacting a higher spiritual power, and the rune chant.

The fourth two lines: *Knowest how one shall send, | knowest how one shall sacrifice?* These final lines link to the "sending" out of the power of the spell when using them for magic (the rune chant will help with this) and for "spending" or dissipating the spell when it has served its purpose. They also advise to neutralize spells cast in an inappropriate manner. Sacrifice here is like that of Odin in the effort exerted in learning all about the rune for magical purposes.

So once you can read the runes, by using these lines we can put together a basic ritual for magical purposes as follows:

- Carving, cutting, or writing of the runes for magical purposes when we know them well enough to do this.
- We paint or stain the symbols required.
- Construct the spell correctly.
- Calling on a higher power
- Chanting or singing the charm
- Sending out the charm, perhaps by burning or sending up with incense
- And lastly to burn the rune charm as is described in Egil's Saga, to spend or dissipate it when it is no longer required.

This ritual can be used for making talismans, carving on wood or bone, or writing on paper. For permanent talismans such as used on jewelry, then you will not be able to use all of the ritual.

Bind Runes

A bind rune is one or more runes put together to enhance the power. A bind rune cannot be thrown together any old way. It should have an aesthetic symmetry, a harmony of the symbols that will blend and work as one. If you find it too difficult to combine two runes, then use them singly and write them next to each other. You might even produce something even more creative than the ones you see here.

A bind rune (as indeed single runes) can be carved into wood, metal, and other materials, or written on parchment or paper, to make talismans.

Here is a travel protection rune of *Algiz* and *Raidho*, see how well they are blended.

Travel Bind Rune

Another rune I have used for business success (depending on the type of business) is a blend of *Fehu* and *Ansuz*.

Business Success Bind rune

Here are some more suggestions: *Algiz* with *Thurisaz* makes a powerful rune of double protection and is a popular combination.

Protection Bind Rune

Tiwaz and *Thurisaz* can bring protection in legal matters.

Legal Protection Bind Rune

Gebo and *Ansuz* is a general good luck rune.

Good Luck Bind Rune

Ansuz and *Mannaz* will provide knowledge and wisdom.

Knowledge and Wisdom Bind Rune

Wunjo and *Sowilo* will bring you joy and happiness.

Joy and Happiness Bind Rune

Some people make a personal rune out of their initials. If your initials are EE, then it is simple in that you can combine, Ehwaz and Ehwaz. For me this would be an ideal rune, as I love to work in a partnership. Partnerships in general are important to me, and exciting journeys of all kinds including metaphorical ones, keep me motivated. However, these are not my initials so I would prefer to combine what I consider to be my personal runes, Ehwaz with Uruz, as my initials make a bind rune that is not agreeable to me. Accordingly, if your initials are HI, then I would think twice about making a personal rune from Hagalaz and Isa. Only do this if your initials correspond with positive runes that mean something personal to you.

If someone gives you a bind rune, then inspect it thoroughly yourself and make sure you agree with it, even they are a skilled runemaster. For instance, let us hypothesize that someone gave you a simple bind rune to help your business. The problem is that you are afraid that as the business is sluggish, you will lose it. The bind rune supplied is combined *Fehu* and *Isa*. The bind rune supplier explains that *Fehu* is to help your prosperity and money earning capabilities and *Isa* is to preserve your business. This might appear logical on first sight. However, would you want to employ *Isa* on its own to help your business prosperity? *Isa* will freeze or block the power of *Fehu*. It will also grip your business in an ice age of goodness knows how long. Better to use *Fehu* by itself, or perhaps use a rune combination to inspire you with innovative ideas to assist your business out of the current slump.

A rule to remember in this is, *if in doubt, do not use!*

Single Runes

I would suggest using single runes to start with. I have given perhaps over simplified examples, as the runes mentioned have more than one meaning. However, I wish to demonstrate simple uses. For instance I use *Ansuz* for my writing inspiration, as for me it is the "writing rune". I use *Fehu* generally for attracting wealth, but it can also be used for fertility. And *Sowilo* is perfect for happiness and success.

Here are some more suggestions:

- *Uruz* will provide inner and outer strength.
- *Ansuz* is for communication
- *Ehwaz* will strengthen partnerships.
- *Algiz* will provide protection.
- *Tiwaz* can be used to succeed in a court case (as long as it is deserved). Slip it in to your shoes or pocket.

Galdr (rune chants)

Galdr is particularly effective for rune charms. They will help you focus and release the magic.

A rune chant should have musical intonation. A chant written with poetical form can also be sung. Many poems have been made into songs. The meditation style chant in particular is perfectly suited to single and bind runes charms and you will find it easier to write. A sound for each rune can be devised, for instance if we want to promote inner and outer strength *Uruz* would be a good choice. In doing so, we can incorporate Norse magical numbers of multiples of three, but particularly three and nine. It is helpful to visualize an associating power animal such as the aurochs or ox.

Here I begin by chanting *Uruz* three times and I also end with this. (I do this with each chant to give them balance). The middle line is also composed of three multiples of three sounds, equaling nine. In this line I chant the first and representative letter U. This can be chanted as "oo" (or "u"). I do this three times and then the second syllable as "ru" or "roo" as it is a softer sound than "ruz", again this is chanted three times, and lastly back to "oo" three times. Each sound should be drawn out to create that softer sound. And they can be sung. Now I have the following chant:

Uruz, Uruz, Uruz
Oo, oo, oo, roo, roo, roo, oo, oo, oo
Uruz, Uruz, Uruz

An alternative chant for *Uruz* would be to draw out the syllables more slowly. This chant as a whole equals nine separate sounds:

Uruz, Uruz, Uruz

Oooooo, rooooo, zzzzzz

Uruz, Uruz, Uruz

For a bind rune, chant each rune one at a time if you are using two runes, otherwise construct one combined chant. Multiples of three runes combined, will create a more powerful charm (three runes = three chants, or three runes = one chant).

Here are some more suggestions for chants:

Fehu

Fehu, Fehu, Fehu
Fe, fe, fe, whoo, whoo, whoo, fe, fe, fe,
Faaaay, whoooo, fraaay
Fehu, Fehu, Fehu

Thurisaz

Thurisaz, Thurisaz, Thurisaz
Th, th, th, thor, thor, thor, th, th, th
Thooor, eeeeee, saaaah
Thurisaz, Thurisaz, Thurisaz

Ansuz

Ansuz, Ansuz, Ansuz
Aaaaaa, nnnnnn, suuuuu
Ansuz, Ansuz, Ansuz
Aaaaaa, nnnnnn, suuuuu
Ansuz, Ansuz, Ansuz

Raidho

Raidho, Raidho, Raidho

Rye, rye, rye, th, th, th, oh, oh oh
Ryyyye, thoooo, ryyyye
Raidho, Raidho, Raidho

Wunjo

Wunjo, Wunjo, Wunjo
Woooon, jooooo, woooon
Wunjo, Wunjo, Wunjo

Gebo

Gebo, Gebo, Gebo
Ge, ga, go, gi, gu, ge
Gggggg, aaayyy, boooow
Gebo, Gebo, Gebo

Algiz

Algiz, Algiz, Algiz
Ahl, ahl, ahl, ahl, ahl, ahl, ahl, ahl, ahl
Aaaahl, geeeee, zzzzzz
Algiz, Algiz, Algiz

Sowilo

Sowilo, Sowilo, Sowilo
Sooooo, weeeee, loooow
Sowilo, Sowilo, Sowilo
Sooooo, weeeee, loooow
Sowilo, Sowilo, Sowilo

Tiwaz

Tiwaz, Tiwaz, Tiwaz
Ti, ti, ti, tyr, tyr, tyr, wah, wah, wah
Tiwaz, Tiwaz, Tiwaz

Ehwaz

Ehwaz, Ehwaz, Ehwaz
Ay, wah, ay, wah, ay, wah
Ehwaz, Ehwaz, Ehwaz
Ay, wah, ay, wah, ay, wah
Ehwaz, Ehwaz, Ehwaz

Rune Candle Magic

Candle magic is a popular form of magic. For centuries candles have been used for divination, in magic, for celebrating and for remembering the dead.

In some Christian church services, two candles are always kept alight as a symbol of goodness and spirituality. Candles are also often placed around coffins and before statues, and lit in remembrance of the dead. It is popular now to hold candlelight vigils for protests and in remembrance. And if someone meets and untimely death, candles are placed in front of photographs along with flowers.

In the more recent past, people decorated Christmas trees with candles (and often caused fires), and indeed were often the only source of light. We still follow the old custom of putting candles on a birthday cake and making a wish and blowing them out. This is a kind of spell. And of course we still have celebratory dinners using candles.

In times past, candles were used for spells and more often than not, love spells. The casting of spells to force a lover to come to you often ended badly and caused unhappiness, as you cannot force someone to love you against their will.

However, candles are more often used for positive magic. A candle is a symbol of light and of the Spirit. It is a correlation of matter and Spirit. The candle flame carries the magic out into the atmosphere and the incense also assists in this, the combination is more powerful than either on its own.

Candles spells are a simple way of inscribing runes. When

constructing a candle spell, choose your candle color carefully as each one means something. You will find color correspondences at the end of the book. Candles can also be used to "offer" as in the *Havamal*. You can light a candle in thanks for help in casting a spell or in thanks of it working.

A note on color

All colors have negative connotations. However, for most spells only the positive values are used. Too much of any one color is not good for you. Try to balance the colors you wear and use in your home. Wearing or using too much of the same color can cause problems such as depleting your energy, inducing depression, or causing discord and confusion. It can also be too overwhelming or underwhelming.

Charms and Spells

Spell for Communication
What you will need:

For this spell you will need a blue candle. Blue relates to communication. It is also a color of harmony.

The rune for communication is *Ansuz*.

For this you can cast a Circle if you wish or make whatever preparations you feel are right. For instance a good time to cast this spell would be during the full moon, and on Odin's day of Wednesday. All positive spells can be cast during the new moon (especially money and new starts), waxing, and full moons.

Prepare yourself with a ritual bath. You can add the same essential oil that you use for candle dressings if you wish, or sea salt, or an essential oil such as frankincense or lavender.

If you wish you could dress your candle as part of the spell and for extra power. Use an essential oil such as sage, eucalyptus, or lavender. The instructions are below. The incense to correspond can be the same as the essential oil.

For carving the rune, use a twig from a magical tree that has been sharpened. I use willow. Otherwise, use a clean, sharp knife that is especially bought and kept for this purpose.

The instructions below pertain to any candle spell, but in each case exchange the chant to suit each rune carved.

Casting the Spell

Find a quiet time and place and prepare your altar table. Ensure you have everything you require, this especially applies if you cast a Circle.

Light any candles you have on your altar (except for the spell candle). Light your incense. Take a few minutes to concentrate on your aims before you begin. Ask for help to empower the spell, you can invoke Odin for instance if you are already practiced at magic, and in this case casting a Circle is wise.

Carve your rune into the center of the candle. Single runes can be carved three times.

Dress the candle with incense oil. Do this with your finger and thumb and work with deosil (clockwise) movements from the center to the top and from the center to the bottom. There are many ways to do this and in this case the power from the candle will be released and directed outwards into the atmosphere. Remember to keep concentrating on your aims.

Now light the candle.

Focus on the candle and concentrate for a few minutes while looking into the flame, then when you are ready chant three times:

Ansuz, Ansuz, Ansuz
Aaaaaa, nnnnnn, suuuuu
Ansuz, Ansuz, Ansuz
Aaaaaa, nnnnnn, suuuuu
Ansuz, Ansuz, Ansuz

Concentrate for a few more minutes.

Now you can either let the candle burn away, or let it burn down one third and then extinguish it. Repeat the spell for two more nights in the three days leading up to the full moon.

Good Luck Spell
What you will need:
A gold (or yellow), or green candle
A blue candle
Orange or Rosemary incense
Orange or Rosemary essential oil
A *Gebo* and *Ansuz* bind rune (or carve separately) as this rune is a traditional good luck combination.

You can chant each rune separately or as a combined chant.

Gebo-Ansuz Chant:
Gebo, Gebo, Gebo
Ge, ga, go, gi, gu, ge
Ggggg, aaayyy, boooow
Gebo, Gebo, Gebo

Ansuz, Ansuz, Ansuz
Aaaaaa, nnnnnn, suuuuu
Ansuz, Ansuz, Ansuz
Aaaaaa, nnnnnn, suuuuu
Ansuz, Ansuz, Ansuz

Combined Chant
Gebo, Ansuz, Gebo
Aaaaaa, gaaaaa, aaaaaa
Ansuz, Gebo, Ansuz
Gaaaaa, aaaaaa, gaaaaa

Gebo, Ansuz, Gebo

Protection Spell
What you will need:
A black candle
A white candle
Frankincense or Black pepper incense
Frankincense or black pepper essential oil
An *Algiz* and *Thurisaz* bind rune (or carve separately)

Algiz-Thurisaz Chant:
Thurisaz, Thurisaz, Thurisaz
Th, th, th, thor, thor, thor, th, th, th
Thooor, eeeeee, saaaah
Thurisaz, Thurisaz, Thurisaz

Algiz, Algiz, Algiz
Ahl, ahl, ahl, ahl, ahl, ahl, ahl, ahl, ahl
Aaaahl, geeeee, zzzzzz
Algiz, Algiz, Algiz

Combined Chant
Algiz, Thurisaz, Algiz
Aaaaal, thooor, geeeee
Thooor, eeeeee, saaaah
Aaaahl, geeeee, zzzzzz
Thooor, aaaaal, thooor
Thurisaz, Algiz, Thurisaz

Strength, Courage, and Direction Spell
What you will need:
Orange Candle
Red candle
Blue candle (place between the others)

Rosemary, Yarrow, Juniper, and Fennel Incense
Yarrow or Fennel Essential oil
A *Tiwaz* and *Uruz* bind rune (or carve separately)

Uruz-Tiwaz Chant

Uruz, Uruz, Uruz
Oooooo, rooooo, zzzzzz
Uruz, Uruz, Uruz
Tiwaz, Tiwaz, Tiwaz
Ti, ti, ti, tyr, tyr, tyr, wah, wah, wah
Tiwaz, Tiwaz, Tiwaz

Combined Chant

Uruz, Tiwaz, Uruz
Oooooo, rooooo, zzzzzz
Ti, ti, ti, tyr, tyr, tyr, wah, wah, wah
Oooooo, rooooo, zzzzzz
Tiwaz, Uruz, Tiwaz

Candle in Bottle Spell

This can be used for all types of spell, changing the colors and messages as necessary.

You will need a clean glass bottle and candle of the appropriate color, for instance pink for friendship, yellow or orange for success. Any bottle will do that will hold a candle (you can shave the end of the candle down). You will also need a magic pen, some ribbon or thread of an appropriate color, parchment or paper, and a bowl containing sand to extinguish the pen. You will also need the usual ritualistic items such as incense. Choose a rune or write a message in runic writing (see below). This spell is cast for three days during the waxing to full moon.

For the magic pen, find some small twigs from a magical tree such as willow, oak, nut-bearing, or an apple tree.

Light the end of the twig and let it burn for a few minutes. You are making charcoal so make sure you do not burn it too much. You can put the flames out in the bowl of sand and check to see if the wood has blackened all the way through. Relight and burn for a little longer if necessary. You can now write magical messages with your pen. When the pen wears down, repeat the process.

Prepare your altar table as before and follow your usual ritual. Dress the candle in essential oil.

Write your message on the paper using runic writing but keep it simple (see below). Roll up the message and tie it with the ribbon (this is necessary as you will want to easily take it out again). Put the message into the bottle. Place the candle in the top of the bottle and light. Staring into the flame, concentrate hard on your wishes for at least nine minutes, and visualize success for the spell.

Repeat for the next two days, but additionally on the third day let the candle burn right through (the bottle will not break). Tip out the message and burn it over the bowl of sand, again while concentrating on your wishes and desires.

How to Make a Rune Wand

A wand is used in ceremony and ritual for focusing and directing magical energy. You can also use it to cast your Circle.

When looking for a rune wand you should use your instincts. A magical wand is made of wood that has magical properties. Popular choices are willow, apple, birch, hazel, or any magical tree or nut wood. If you have made wooden runes then I would suggest using the same sort of wood. Try to find as straight a piece of wood as possible.

The recommended length for a rune wand is from your elbow to your middle finger tip or about 45 cm (18 inches). The width should be large enough to carve your rune symbols on but not too wide that it is hard to wield. At least the width or double the width of your index finger will suffice.

You may have read that you should cut a wand from a hazel

tree of not more than one-year's new growth, at dawn, on a Wednesday, and so forth. On the other hand, this is rarely possible for various reasons. This is where your instincts come in. I obtained my wand from a very old and beautiful weeping willow. It had a natural handle and when I measured it I did not include the handle.

Try to use a windfall piece of wood, rather than take it from a living tree, and bide your time when looking for it. After you have your wood, if you can identify the tree from which it came, leave an offering. Otherwise leave your gift at the tree closest to where you found it. An offering can simply be water or a crystal buried at the root.

Once you have your wood leave it as it is unless the bark is flaky. The bark still remains on my wand after many years and still looks the same. Do not varnish or add chemicals of any kind to the wand as it will block or destroy the natural energy. Look at the beauty of the natural wood. Nothing needs to be added except the rune symbols. Try not to add anything extra. To add fripperies will only disguise the natural beauty and is unnecessary.

Carve all the rune symbols in order on the wand; on some wood it is possible to draw them. You can do this within a Sacred Circle and with a dedicated ceremony. Cleanse and empower your wand in the same way as you have or would the runes as shown in Chapter 6.

Rune Wheel

An alternative to a rune wand is a rune wheel. Keep it simple and carve the rune symbols around the outer rim or if you are drawing it (which is simpler); again write them on the outer rim. It should have eight spokes which represent the eight runes of each aett. Eight also represents the cycles of nature and the eight natural pagan festivals of two solstices and two equinoxes, and the major festivals of Samhain, Imbolc, Beltane, and Lammas.

You can carry or wear the runic wheel as a powerful talisman.

In addition you can use it in magic or give it a central place on your altar or work table.

Rune Wheel

Runic Writing

Runic writing can be used for magical messages. Below is the way I do it. All letters are included in the rune meanings. The following rules will apply as some letters will be missing and there are extra sounds as in diphthongs. Remember that you are writing English words in "Runic" letters. It will also depend on how you pronounce the letters, and these differ from writer to writer who will possibly take the pronunciations from Primitive Norse or Old Norse, and some whom ignore accented sounds:

A is *Ansuz*
B is *Berkano*

C use K *Kenaz*

D is *Dagaz*

E is *Ehwaz*

F is *Fehu*

G is *Gebo*

H is *Hagalaz*

I is *Isa*

J is *Jera*

K is *Kenaz*

L is *Laguz*

M is *Mannaz*

N is *Nauthiz*

O is *Othala*

P is Perthro

Q use *Kenaz*

R is *Raidho*

S is *Sowilo*

T is *Tiwaz*

U is *Uruz*

V use *Wunjo*

W is *Wunjo*

X use KS *Kenaz/Sowilo* or possibly GS *Gebo/Sowilo* (depending on the sound and it would be unlikely you will want to begin a word with X such as xylophone), therefore X in fox and sex would be foks and seks, examination would be eks-a-min-ay-tjon (tion), egs-a-min-ay-tjon (tion). This is rather long winded and ambiguous, so I would use the abbreviation "exams" which becomes "egsams" or eksams".

Y use *Jera*

Z is *Algiz*

For **TH** sounds (as in thought) use *Thurisaz*

For **EI** you can use *Eihwaz*

For **NG** sounds (as in wishing) use one runic letter, *Ingwaz*

For **CH** (church) use T, J and **SH** (wish) use S, J (although some writers keep to the C, H or S, H as there is not one sound for these). "Wish" would be "w-i-s-j" or "w-i-s-h".

So if you want to write "luck and happiness" or "success and happiness" First you write it phonetically "luk and hapines" or "sukses and hapines" and then transfer this into runes.

S U K S E S   A N D   H A P I N E S

Success and Happiness Message

You will find there is much ambiguity as with writing "examination". If you become stuck, then try to think of an alternative word for what you want to say, as I did with "exams". An alternative for final examinations would be "finals" or simple examination "class test".

Remember all the advice about Magic. Practice makes perfect but start with simple things and gradually build it up. As you come to know the runes you will begin to make your own bond with them, and they will guide you on your journey along life's pathway.

Appendix

Gods and Goddesses of the Northern Pantheon

Odin

Odin is the chief Norse god, and the All-Father. He is the son of Bor and Bestla. Together with Frigg, his children are Baldur, Hod, and Hermod, and he also fathered Thor by the goddess Jord. In Old-English he is known as Woden, and the day of the week Wednesday, is named after him.

A formidable figure, Odin is the god of kings, nobles, poets, the dead, war, warriors, magic and wisdom. He is also a teacher and a healer, but has a strong sexuality. He is a shape-shifter and loves disguise. A tall man he is often seen walking the earth dressed in a blue cloak, and a wide-brimmed hat, and has long hair and a beard. He resides in his hall Valhalla in Asgard, where warriors killed in battle are taken.

He only has one eye as he gave the other at the well of Mimir in return for a drink which gave him wisdom and inspiration. And he hung for nine days from the world tree, without food or drink and pierced by his own spear, until he saw the runes below him and scooped them up gaining knowledge of them. He is connected to the *Ansuz* rune.

Odin has a spear Gungnir, which always reaches its target, a ring Draupnir, and an eight-footed horse, Sleipnir. Two wolves Freki and Geri, and two ravens Hugin (thought) and Mugin (memory), are his companions.

He is the father of the Aesir gods but also the father of humankind. After slaying the giant Ymir, he and his two brothers, Vili and Ve, fashioned the universe (heavens, middle earth, and the underworld) from his bones, blood, and flesh. Out of two logs

Ash and the Elm, Odin and his brothers created two people, and gave them life and they became man and woman, Ask and Embla.

At Ragnarok, Odin is destined to die after being swallowed by the wolf Fenrir.

Thor

Thor is the Norse god of thunder and storms. He is son of Odin, and Jord the earth goddess. His wife is Sif the gold-haired fertility goddess, and his mistress Jarnsaxa. He has three children in all, two sons Magni and Modi and one daughter, Thrud. Thursday is named after him hailing from the Old-English. Thor is the god of thunder, lightening, wind, rain, farmers and sailors, and is also a god of war. His rune is *Thurisaz*. Thor lives in the palace Bilskirnir located in Asgard, with Sif and his children.

Usually portrayed as a giant of a man, Thor is usually seen with red hair and beard and with eyes ablaze with lightening. He has a mighty hammer called Mjollnir, which magically returns to him after being thrown. His wears the belt Megingjard, which doubles his already formidable strength and has a pair of iron gauntlets. He travels across the heavens in his chariot drawn by the goats, Tanngrisni and Tanngjnostr.

He is more often than not portrayed as having dull wits, and was deceived and tormented by Loki who was jealous of him. Thor was cunning though and lived by his actions rather than words.

At Ragnarok, Thor will kill the Midgard serpent Jormungand, but will die from its poison.

Tyr

Tyr is the god of war and justice and was the chief god before Odin. Tyr keeps his pledges and has great honor. He is bold and courageous. His valor and heroism inspires others. In Old-English the day of the week Tuesday, is named after him. His rune is *Tiwaz* and his spear is a symbol of Justice.

Tyr is missing a hand, and this is told in the myth about the chaining of the wolf Fenrir, who eventually is the downfall of Odin. Fenrir posed a threat to the gods, and after trying many chains, they had the magical fetter Gleipnir forged by the dwarfs, and tricked him into testing out his strength on it. Distrustful, Fenrir would only agree if one of the gods put his hand in his mouth. None stepped forward except Tyr. When Fenrir could not break free from the chain, the gods mocked him, but Tyr remained where he was and waited for the wolf to take his revenge and duly lost his hand.

Tyr is destined at Ragnarok to kill but be killed by the hound Garm the guardian of Hel.

Frey

Frey (meaning Lord) is the god of fertility, sun, rain, and the patron of the bountiful harvest. He is the ruler of Alfheim, the land of the light elves. He is the son of Njord and brother of Freyja and is of the Vanir gods. However, as a token of peace he and his sister, together with their father, were sent to join the Aesir gods. He has a golden boar Gullinbursti, which can pull a chariot or be ridden. He owns a ship called Skidbladnir, which always sails straight to where it is directed and can be folded up so small it fits into a pocket or pouch. His sword is magical and leaps from its sheaf and fight battles on its own, reaping carnage whenever and wherever it is needed.

Frey fell in love with Gerd daughter of the Gymir the frost giant. But his wooing went in vain. He asked his servant Skirnir to help him persuade her to be his wife. Skirnir agreed and Frey surrendered the magical sword to him as a reward. Gerd refused Skirnir's bribes, so Skirnir accomplished his task by using magical runes and Frey won her love (albeit by magic). Unfortunately, the consequences of giving away his magic sword will cause his destruction, and Frey will be killed at Ragnarok by the fire giant Surt.

Freyja

Freyja (meaning Lady), Bride of the Vanir, is the goddess of fertility, sensuality, love, beauty, music and childbirth. She is sister to Frey, and daughter of Njord. She is famed for her beauty and her counterparts are Venus and Aphrodite in the Roman and Greek myths respectively. She is also known as a sorceress as she is skilled in magic, especially that of seidhr. It is said that on joining the Aesir, she instructed Odin in the magical arts.

Freyja is young and full of life. She is fertile and ripe for pregnancy. Although filled with love and energy, she is also the battle goddess with much strength. She is married to the god Odr, but he left her to travel to faraway lands. Missing him, Freyja cried teardrops of gold and amber. Also associated with war and death, she claims half of all battle slain warriors with Odin, half going to Valhalla and half going to her own hall.

Freyja has a magical cloak of feathers, which allows the wearer to change into a falcon. She rides a chariot, which is pulled by two large cats. In one myth, Freyja asked four dwarfs to make her a necklace of amber and gold (called Brisingamen), but they would only agree if she slept with all of them, which she did.

As Freyja is married to Odr, there are claims that this is Odin and that she and Frigg are one and the same goddess, but there are more claims that dispute this.

Frigg

Frigg is the goddess of marriage, childbirth, motherhood, and the household. She is also known as a love and fertility goddess, and is another reason she and Freyja are claimed to be one goddess. She is the foremost goddess of the Aesir. Friday from the Old-English is named after her (though some say it is Freyja). Frigg is wise and has the power of prophecy.

Frigg is the wife of Odin and joins him in the wild hunt. Her children are Baldur and Hod, although some sources add Wecta.

Frigg tried to prevent the death of her son Baldur, after he kept dreaming of it. Wanting to protect her son from peril, she obtained oaths from every creature and object in nature, that they would never harm Baldur, but alas overlooked the mistletoe. Baldur was later killed by a dart of mistletoe, thrown by the blind Hod, but instigated by Loki the trickster god.

Baldur

Baldur the fairest and best loved, is the god of light, purity, joy, innocence, and beauty. He is the son of Odin and Frigg. He is good and wise. His wife is Nanna, and his daughter is Nep and his son is Forseti (god of justice).

Baldur had been dreaming about his own death. His mother Frigg obtained oaths from fire, water, all kinds of metal, earth, stones, poison, ailments, serpents, all beasts, trees and plants, in fact from every creature and object in nature, asking that they never harm him, alas she overlooked the mistletoe as being too insignificant. The gods thought him invincible and enjoyed using him for target practice.

Loki was jealous of Baldur, and disguising himself as a woman, asked Frigg if indeed nothing could harm Baldur. Frigg told him only the mistletoe as she thought it too young to be concerned about. Loki went back to the assembly and tricked Baldur's brother the blind Hod by suggesting he join in the target practice and providing him with the weapon. The unsuspecting Hod with the help of Loki, threw a dart of mistletoe and it struck Baldur killing him, and thus depriving gods and humankind alike of this wonderful god.

Odin sent another one of his sons Hermod to the goddess Hel of the underworld, to plead for his life back. Hel agreed but only if everyone wept for Baldur. Everyone agreed todo so except Loki, and so Baldur had to remain in the Underworld. Baldur's wife Nanna died of a broken heart and was placed next to him on his funeral pyre.

Unfortunately, Hod was killed in revenge by his brother Vali (rather unfairly), and Loki ran away and hid himself but he was discovered and escaped with only a terrible punishment. He was bound and a poisonous snake fastened above his head dripping its poison on him. He was to stay thus until Ragnarok.

At Ragnarok, both Baldur and Hod will be reborn.

Loki

Loki is a god of chaos, fire and magic and is a shape-shifter, and he seems lacking in the nicer qualities and does tend to get a lot of bad press. He is the son of two giants. Although he is cunning and a trickster, he is also heroic and often worked with the other gods and goddesses. However this was often in having to put his misdeeds right after leading the gods into dangerous situations. Early on in the myths his deeds were more mischievous than malicious.

He was married to the goddess Sigyn by whom he had two sons Narvi and Vali (not to be confused with Vali a son of Odin), and had a mistress Angrboda by whom he had Fenrir the wolf (that is destined to kill Odin at Ragnarok), Jormungand the serpent, and the goddess Hel. He also gave birth to Sleipnir Odon's eight-legged horse after turning into a mare and sleeping with a stallion.

As time went on Loki became more and more malicious and sinister and was often jealous of the other gods, and none more so than Baldur. After causing the death of Baldur and being captured, his son Vali was turned into a vicious wolf and immediately set upon and devoured his other son Narvi. Narvi's entrails were used to bind Loki.

At Ragnarok, Loki will free himself and lead his three offspring in the forces of evil against the gods. He will kill and be killed by Heimdall.

Heimdall

Heimdall is god of light, the watcher of the gods and guardian of

Bifrost the Rainbow Bridge. He is the son of nine mothers and is sometimes called Rig and is said to be the father of all people on earth made up of the serfs, peasants, and the warriors or nobles. Because of this he is linked to the rune *Mannaz* but perhaps as a guardian also *Algiz*.

Heimdall has the gift of prophecy and has amazing vision, and hearing so acute he can hear grass grow and he needs less sleep than a bird. Heimdall is a good and peaceful god. Once he helped Freyja find her necklace Brisingamen after it was stolen by Loki. They fought and Heimdall won returning the necklace to Freyja.

He will blow his horn Gjallarhorn to signal the onset of Ragnarok where he and the god Loki are destined to kill each other.

Glossaries

Glossary of the Psyche

Collective Unconscious

The collective unconscious is part of the unconscious and is like a reservoir of accumulated psychological inheritance that runs through all of humanity. It is inherited from primitive times and through centuries past, and embraces all cultures. We share with other people these inherited archetypes and themes. They live on through us and will be passed down to our descendants.

There are two sides to the unconscious, *the personal unconscious* where we store things we do not need for now or things we want to forget, and the *collective unconscious* (which we share with everyone). It is a spiritual understanding.

The Vikings would agree with this view as they believed the burdens of our ancestors are carried in our genes. Tapping into the unconscious can reveal our innermost hopes and fears. It is the bright side of life and the dark side of life. Jung calls these the *Anima* and *Animus* which we must get in touch with along with the *Shadow* before we can truly get in touch with the *Self*. Getting in touch with the Anima/Animus can prove valuable as they can act as a messenger between the conscious and the unconscious, linking the two as the runes do.

Archetypes

Archetype is a word that was used by Jung to describe certain features of psychology especially in relation to the collective unconscious. Archetypes are symbolic images or motifs buried deep in the unconscious and which exist outside time and space. We share archetypes with all other people.

Jung studied Astrology, the I Ching, and Tarot, and many

other ancient mysteries such as the Mandala. Archetypal examples would be such things as *the nurturing mother, the hero, the old hermit, the Divine child,* and *the young seductress*, which often appear in dreams and which he believed formed the basis of religion, myth, and art.

Anima/Animus

The *anima* is the unconscious or inner feminine aspect of a man's personality, while the *animus* is the unconscious or inner male aspect of the woman's, in other words your gender opposite. They are both archetypes of the unconscious mind and can appear in dreams. The anima often appears as a single female, such as a seductress or Spirit Guide and is the feeling part of a man's psyche and associated with water or earth. The animus appears often as a hero or poet and is the logical and thinking part of a woman's psyche and associated with fire and air. The anima and animus draw power from the collective unconscious.

Getting in touch with your anima or animus can be valuable in connecting your conscious with your unconscious.

Ego

The ego is the center of consciousness (or who we are). It is our sense of identity. We get to know our ego-consciousness, by becoming familiar with our strengths and weaknesses. An inflated ego is counterproductive to the discovery of the *Self* or *Individuation*.

Shadow

The shadow is the unconscious part of us that contains our weaknesses. It is the darker side of us, and is often repressed by us. It can appear in our dreams as a dark or ominous person of our own sex. If we confront and accept our shadow, it can be the first step to individuation. This step into the discovery of the Self must not be skipped over or even missed as it is an essential part of the psyche. However, it is not easy to face up to and accept so we have to take courage in doing so.

The Self and Individuation

The Self is the archetype of the totality of the entire psyche. It draws its power from the collective unconscious and is often symbolized as a mandala or circle and connected to the number four. The Self is not easily accepted by the ego.

Individuation is the discovery of the Self, by realization and through a balancing of the psyche. Through Individuation the person becomes closer to the Self and as a result becomes less selfish, and so more social, and more of an individual.

Color Correspondences

White
Moon, purity, peace, truth, creativity, new ventures, divine inspiration, attracting positive energy, protection
Black
Protection, acceptance, change, grounding, banishing negativity, the shadow self
Gold
Sun, Higher spirituality, happiness, attraction, luck, money, inner strength, creativity
Silver
Moon, secret dreams, intuition, clairvoyance, protection, goddess, astral energy
Blue
Water, empathy, peace, healing, harmony, honesty, wisdom, spiritual matters, communication, intuition, loyalty
Red
Fire, vitality, potency, energy, passion, love, sexuality, power, courage, survival, strength, motivation

Yellow

Air, sun, happiness, optimism, communication, luck, confidence, creativity, attraction, careers, imagination, success

Purple

Psychic awareness, clairvoyance, magic, spiritual energy and growth, dreams, astral projection, inner happiness, wisdom

Pink

Love, friendship, affection, fidelity, devotion, honor, health, family, binding

Green

Earth, Romantic love, healing, fertility, money, good luck, abundance, growth, beauty, harvest, agriculture

Orange

Confidence, optimism, ambition, success, strength, creativity, energy, stamina, career, goals, legal matters

Brown

Earth, home, practical matters, animal healing, endurance, harvest, lost objects, legal matters

Grey

Uncertainty, confusion, tiredness, neutrality, stalemate, both absorbing and repelling (as black and white blend)

B O O K S

O is a symbol of the world, of oneness and unity. In different cultures it also means the "eye," symbolizing knowledge and insight. We aim to publish books that are accessible, constructive and that challenge accepted opinion, both that of academia and the "moral majority."

Our books are available in all good English language bookstores worldwide. If you don't see the book on the shelves ask the bookstore to order it for you, quoting the ISBN number and title. Alternatively you can order online (all major online retail sites carry our titles) or contact the distributor in the relevant country, listed on the copyright page.

See our website **www.o-books.net** for a full list of over 500 titles, growing by 100 a year.

And tune in to myspiritradio.com for our book review radio show, hosted by June-Elleni Laine, where you can listen to the authors discussing their books.

MySpiritRadio